32 LOW-COST HOME-BASED BUSINESSES

32
Low-Cost
Home-Based
Businesses

BY THE EDITORS OF

Income
OPPORTUNITIES

PRENTICE HALL
Englewood Cliffs, New Jersey 07632

Prentice-Hall International (UK) Limited, *London*
Prentice-Hall of Australia Pty. Limited, *Sydney*
Prentice-Hall Canada, Inc., *Toronto*
Prentice-Hall Hispanoamericana, S.A., *Mexico*
Prentice-Hall of India Private Limited, *New Delhi*
Prentice-Hall of Japan, Inc., *Tokyo*
Simon & Schuster Asia Pte. Ltd., *Singapore*
Editora Prentice-Hall do Brasil, Ltda., *Rio de Janeiro*

© 1992 by
Prentice-Hall, Inc.
Englewood Cliffs, NJ

10 9 8 7 6 5 4 3 2 1

Library of Congress Cataloging-in-Publication Data
32 low-cost home-based businesses / by the editors of
Income opportunities.
   p.   cm.
Includes index.
ISBN 0-13-919010-4
1. Income opportunities. 2. New business enterprises.
I. Income opportunities. II. Title: Thirty-two low-cost
home-based businesses.
HD2333.A14 1992   92-19694
658'.041—dc20   CIP

ISBN 0-13-919010-4

PRENTICE HALL
Professional Publishing
Englewood Cliffs, NJ 07632
Simon & Schuster. A Paramount Communications Company

Printed in the United States of America

CONTENTS

Preface: About This Book

Acknowledgments

How to Use This Book

ABOUT THIS BOOK

The volume you hold in your hands was compiled, edited, and produced by the editors, staff, and contributors of INCOME OPPORTUNITIES magazine, one of the most respected publications of its kind. Over thirty-five years of experience and research have gone into the making of this publication to help make it, perhaps, one of the most valuable books you have ever purchased.

There is no doubt that you could have learned all that is contained in this book from your own research. But how long would it have taken you ... months? Years? And how much would it have cost you in time and materials? Far more than the price of this book.

It is far better that you direct your time and energy toward the establishment and building of your new part-time business — and this book is designed to provide you with the ideas and the start-up information you need.

ACKNOWLEDGMENTS

We would like to gratefully acknowledge the contributions of the following authors: William Ball, David Boyd, Van Caldwell, Ron Coleman, R.T. Edwards, Louis Epstein, Eric Gibson, Lee Harbert, William Harrel, Patricia J. Hazlett, Laurel Holliday, Wendy Hopps, Priscilla Y. Huff, Mildred Jailer, H.K. King, Art Lamons, Ken Larkman, Thomas J. Lucier, Adeline McConnell, Paula Nichols, Denise Osburn, Gary D. Plummer, Silvia Shepard, Jo Ann M. Unger, and Perry Wilbur; and the following editors: Stephen Wagner, Arthur Blougouras, and Jannean Bryant.

HOW TO USE
THIS BOOK

The format of this book is designed to make it as simple as possible for you to find a home-based business and then put it into operation. It is our intention to eliminate or minimize much of the doubt, confusion, and guesswork that is often involved in any business start-up.

The first three parts of this book provide general start-up information that is applicable for just about any business. The last three parts detail more than thirty suggested home-based businesses based on actual case histories. Before you choose (or adapt) one, read the case histories carefully to get an overall view of the particular business in which you are interested. You'll get a pretty good idea of the costs involved, the work required, the advantages, and the drawbacks — all before you make your first move. When you have chosen an idea, then refer to the basic start-up information. Then you can begin the foundation of your own home-based business. It is not mandatory that you follow each step exactly as we have presented them here; they are only meant as guides to help you find the easiest, quickest route to success.

Part One:

ESTABLISH
YOUR BUSINESS

NOW IS THE TIME TO START

If you've considered starting a home business but hesitated because of doubts about your ability to succeed, you may want to reconsider. Home-based businesses have a higher survival rate than other types of new ventures, according to a major national study of business start-ups. Sponsored by the National Federation of Independent Business (NFIB) and American Express Company, the three-year study of 2,994 new businesses and their owners found that 82 percent of the home businesses were still in existence after three years, while the rate for all types of new ventures was 77 percent.

The survey results suggest that previous studies may have generally underestimated the success rate of new businesses. The NFIB/American Express three-year survival figure of 77 percent is somewhat higher than estimates by the Small Business Administration, for example, that less than half of all new firms are in existence after five years.

Home-based businesses made up 7 percent of the start-ups analyzed. The home enterprises were less likely to add employees than other new firms, but their operations were more stable, and they appeared better able to weather the inevitable setbacks encountered by new businesses.

These businesses also didn't fit the theory that undercapitalization is the kiss of death for a new venture, even a very small one. The companies that started with capital of $50,000 or more had a survival rate of 82 percent. In contrast, nearly a third of the businesses in the study began with $10,000 or less; they had a 75 percent success rate.

According to the survey, the key characteristics of a successful home business operator include the following:

- *Working long hours.* New business owners need to put in long hours to make their ventures succeed. Nearly 80 percent of the entrepreneurs who worked between sixty and seventy-nine hours a week were successful; the survival rate dropped for those who worked more or less than that.

- *Being confident of success.* The would-be entrepreneur shouldn't underestimate the truth of the cliché that confidence breeds success. The study found that the more optimistic about success the owner was, the more likely the business was to survive and grow; 83 percent of the entrepreneurs who rated their odds of success at nine out of ten survived the three-year start-up period. In contrast, those who rated their odds at five out of ten had a survival rate of only 67 percent.

- *Knowing your product or service.* Drawing on your background and experience for a business idea increases your chances of success. Of the owners surveyed, 43 percent said the idea for their enterprise came from a previous job, and 18 percent from a hobby or personal interest. These businesses were more likely to grow than those in which the idea was not directly related to the entrepreneur's personal knowledge.

- *Devoting full time to the business.* Business owners who try to "serve two masters" by operating a venture while holding down another job reduce their chances of success. The owners who devoted full time to their companies had a 78 percent survival rate, eight points higher than those who also worked at another job.

- *Stressing service rather than price.* Emphasizing service instead of price is another trademark of the successful start-ups. The enterprises whose strategy focused on quality service had an 82 percent survival rate, while the rate was twelve points lower for those competing primarily on price. "The idea that customers always chase low prices is clearly unfounded," says William J. Dennis, the NFIB's senior researcher. "Good service is just good business strategy."

In profiling the typical successful small-business entrepreneur, the survey found that he or she was thirty-five years old and married to a working spouse. The owner started the company without relocating and had worked at no more than five other jobs before going into business.

Nearly a quarter of the business owners in the study were women, a figure that would have been higher if part-time businesses had been included. Their success rate was somewhat lower than that of their male counterparts: 71 percent versus 78 percent.

One surprising finding of the survey involved franchises, whose advocates contend that the proven methods and name recognition of such operations increase the entrepreneur's odds of survival. The NFIB/American Express analysis found that this was not necessarily the case. Businesses with a high percentage of their sales coming from franchised goods or services tended to have lower employment growth, and there was no clear-cut link between owning a franchise and business success; 78 percent of the businesses operating under a franchise name survived the start-up period just one point higher than the overall rate in the study.

What inspired these business people to take the biggest risk of their lives? Less than half said their primary motivation was financial. More than 70 percent cited reasons dealing with personal satisfaction, such as "greater control over my life," "using my skills and abilities," and "building something for my family."

Significantly, even with the benefit of three years of hindsight, 82 percent said they would start the same business again, although about half of them would make a major change in the way they did it. Only three percent were so disappointed with the experience that they would never go into business again.

PART- OR FULL-TIME

When beginning their own home businesses, many people ask if they should start on a part-time basis or jump into it full-time. Without a doubt, it is best to start slow. Don't quit your regular job just yet. What if you are currently unemployed? Believe it or not, unless you are retired, it is recommended that you first find full-time work to support yourself and your family while beginning your home-based business—or any home-based business for that matter—part-time.

Starting on a part-time basis has many advantages:

- It gives you the peace of mind that comes with a steady paycheck coming in from your regular job and the ability to put food on the table and pay the bills.

- It allows you to experiment with several methods of operation and types of promotion until you find the right combination that brings in the clients and yields profits.

- It keeps your investment to a minimum.

- You may find that you never want to operate on a full-time basis, that you are satisfied with the part-time income that your sideline business will generate.

- Starting small allows you to learn about every facet of your business and to make mistakes without devastating consequences.

Are there advantages to starting on a full-time basis, if the business lends itself to full-time operation? First of all, even to consider such a plunge, you'd have to be certain that you could handle it financially. If you have a lot of money to play around with and providing for your family is not a worry, then you might want to give it a shot. The advantage here is that your full-time concentration and devoted energy to your new business might bring about greater success more quickly. Notice, even here we say "might," since there are no guarantees.

We recommend starting part-time. Get to know the business, learn all the ins and outs, and experiment with various operational techniques and promotion strategies. Take your time. Your growing profits will tell you when it's time to go full-time, if that's what you want. And who knows, it may be sooner than you imagine.

CHOOSE THE BEST BUSINESS FOR YOU

One of the keys to the success of your home-based business is knowing which is right for you to start in the first place. It is vital to determine which business interests you the most—one you'll enjoy working at—and that fits your particular background and experience. Remember, a business that is potentially profitable does not mean that it will fit your personal needs or that you will like it.

Many entrepreneurs seek advice from friends and relatives. The problem with this approach is that if you ask ten different people, you'll get ten different answers. Eight will give you different ideas that "can't lose," and the other two will think you're totally crazy for wanting your own business at all.

Here are thirteen criteria for your proposed business that you should consider as they may relate to your personality, background, habits, and likes and dislikes. If you have not yet chosen any business for consideration, return to this section when you have. If you are trying to decide among two or more businesses, see which one ranks best against these criteria:

1. **Income Potential.** Can the prospective business produce the amount of income you want? The first consideration you should make is how much money you *want* to earn, not what you need. If a business is providing only enough income to provide for your needs and not your wants, you won't be satisfied. If the majority of your competitors don't make the kind of income you hope to make, don't assume that your operation will be that much better.

2. **Sales Calls.** If you don't enjoy making sales calls, don't consider a business that requires you to be an aggressive salesperson. Many peo-

ple don't know their true feelings with respect to sales calls. If this is true for you, take a part-time or evening job in which you have to make sales calls. You will find out rather quickly if this is for you. All businesses require you to sell, in one way or another. Selling via mail order requires no personal contact, while direct selling requires lots of one-on-one contact.

3. **Morning or Night Person.** Do you greet the early morning with energy and enthusiasm? Or do you hate getting up early? If the latter is true, you should avoid businesses which may require you to be up and alert far earlier than your clients. It is very important to fit the hours of the business to your built-in body clock rather than vice-versa. If you must totally change your lifestyle, the chances are that in time you will grow to resent and even hate what you are doing.

4. **Employees.** Most home businesses don't require employees other than yourself, but some do. Running a business that requires managing an assistant or two necessitates more effort than a business that only you and perhaps your spouse operate.

5. **Nights and Weekends.** Does the prospective business require that you work both nights *and* weekends? Many home-based businesses do require this extra effort. If you are used to recreation and outings with family and friends each weekend, you may resent putting all of

this time into your new endeavor. However, some businesses (like custom catering) make most of their money on weekends. Are you ready to make this kind of commitment?

6. **Status.** What are your feelings about your own status in the community? If status is important to you, does your new enterprise afford this status? Does it detract from it?

7. **Family Working with You.** Are you planning to have your family assist you? Do they support the idea and are they willing? The time to discuss this aspect of your planning is *before* you make a change, not after.

8. **Special Training.** Will you need to re-train yourself in order to run your new business? Is the cost and time involved worth the end result? Many people feel that they can't learn new skills or ideas. If this is your feeling, consider only an idea that falls within your current scope of knowledge.

9. **Long Hours.** If you have a regular job, a business that you run at home may eat up all your spare time. Can you handle this major change in your lifestyle? Can you physically take the greater workload? Will you resent those extra hours?

10. **Future Potential.** Have you examined the full potential of the proposed business? Is the market expanding and increasing for the product or service? Or is it just a fad that may fade away in a few years—or a few months?

11. **Physical Stamina.** Some businesses require a degree of physical stamina. Do you have any physical ailments which will hamper this?

12. **Dealing with People.** Most businesses require contact with people; after all, it is people who buy your product or service. Some are nice, others not so nice. If you don't like dealing with people, perhaps a mail order operation is better suited to you.

13. **Control Your Own Hours.** Is it important to control your own operational hours? If so, you may not like a business in which your hours are dictated by the convenience of your clients.

THE BUSINESS STRUCTURE

There are essentially three forms of business: the sole proprietorship, the partnership, and the corporation. Most likely, you will be supplying your own money to start your business and so will be operating as a "sole proprietor." But if later you need extra capital, or if the business gets too big for one person to handle, you might consider taking on a partner. It is unlikely that you will incorporate your home-based business, but some people do.

When that decision does face you, you'll want to be aware of the advantages and disadvantages of each form of doing business. Each has different applications regarding taxes, management, liability of the owner, and distribution of profits. When you do make a decision, you will naturally want to discuss your options with your accountant or your lawyer, but in order to save yourself some time, you will want at least a basic knowledge of the different legal forms of business ownership.

The Sole Proprietorship

As its name implies, a sole proprietorship is owned by one individual. It is the easiest to start and the least complicated to dissolve. If you are a sole proprietor, you have plenty of company: almost three out of four businesses are owned in this manner. And you all share a number of advantages:

1. You own all the profits. No other form of organization allows one person to own 100 percent of the profits earned by the business.

2. Your business is easy and cheap to organize. You don't need any government approval, although you may be required to carry a city, state, or county license. But these customarily involve only paying a few dollars and the simple formality of signing an application. Your only other obligation is to notify your state for the purposes of collecting sales tax, if any.

3. You're the boss. As a sole proprietor, you have the maximum amount of freedom in managerial decisions. You can expand or condense your business as you see fit; you may sell or close at will; you may change from one kind of business to another, as you wish. In addition, you can make such decisions promptly without having to consult with others.

4. You enjoy certain tax savings. You must pay regular individual taxes on your income, property, and payroll, but these are not levied as special taxes, as with a corporation. You will also have to pay sales tax that you will receive from your customers.

5. You benefit from greater personal incentive and satisfaction. Since you have your investment to lose if your business is not successful, you should be more willing to put time, thought, and energy into the business. And when your business *is* successful, you enjoy maximum sense of accomplishment.

6. You will usually enjoy a better credit standing. Since your creditors can attach your personal wealth, if necessary, they usually will be quicker to extend additional credit to a sole proprietor than to a corporation of equal size and value. The exception would be if you own no other assets beyond your business.

7. You can go out of business more easily. The business automatically ends when you stop doing it, with no legal complications or procedures other than paying off any indebtedness.

As rosy a picture as this paints of the sole proprietorship, there are a few disadvantages:

1. You incur unlimited liability. Practically everything you own is subject to liquidation for the purpose of paying your business debts. If you stop doing business, and your business assets

are not enough to offset any debts, your creditors can attach your personal assets to collect.

2. You are limited as to growth. You may have to
change to another form of ownership in order
to grow as large as you desire.

3. One of the companions to total ownership is
total responsibility. You may have to handle
some business responsibilities that you have
never encountered before.

4. Your business ends with your death or other
incapacity. Even though others might attempt
to keep the business going, the loss of the individual who started and nourished it will usually result in its closing, even when continued
under a new owner.

Don't let these few possible drawbacks deter you, however. For the part-time business, they are not usually factors.

Since you will almost certainly begin as a sole proprietor, you can skip to the next section of this chapter, Name
Your Business. The following information about other
forms of ownership is provided for possible future reference.

Partnership

Often, the first thought toward changing the form of
business occurs when the sole proprietor considers taking
on a partner (or partners). The question might come up
because you need additional capital, or because a valued
employee is no longer content to be just an employee and

is thinking of opening his own competing business. So in order to raise the needed money, or to keep from losing that employee, you start thinking "partners."

Like the sole proprietorship, the partnership is easily started, although it is highly recommended that a partnership agreement be drawn up by a lawyer to prevent future misunderstandings. Also, the partnership shares a similar tax situation, but there are additional advantages that pertain to the partnership alone:

1. You have access to a greater amount of capital. Instead of being limited to one person's personal worth, you can double, triple, or even further multiply that capital by taking on additional partners or one wealthy partner.

2. You enjoy a higher credit standing. Like the sole proprietor, a partner's personal wealth is also available to satisfy business debts. But since there are two personal estates available, the partnership will usually seem a much better risk to creditors.

3. You have more than one "brain" to handle management problems. If the partners complement each other, each one suited to different aspects of the business, progress can be accelerated by their combined knowledge and ability. Also, having someone to consult on business matters can help you make wiser decisions.

Naturally, the partnership form of doing business has its share of disadvantages, many of them similar to the sole proprietorship. Among them are unlimited liability for all partners (regardless of which one makes the bad decisions), growth limited to the amount of capital the partners can raise, and automatic dissolution of the business in the event of the death or incapacitation of one of the partners.

But perhaps the biggest drawback to partnerships is the susceptibility of the partners to disagreements over basic business policies. Even if these disagreements do not cause the business to close, bad feelings can make daily operation difficult for everyone concerned. To have any chance at success, partners must be compatible and seek a common goal.

The Corporation

The third business structure commonly employed by small business is the corporation, a legal entity with the rights, duties, and powers of a person. As its owners change, the corporation keeps the same identity. Although commonly associated with huge conglomerates, a business doesn't have to be a large organization to incorporate. There are, in fact, many small business corporations. But like other forms of business, the corporation has its own advantages and disadvantages:

1. You risk only the money you invest in the corporation.
2. There is no limit to your growth potential.
3. You can easily transfer ownership.
4. Your business can go on indefinitely.

On the other hand, there are definite disadvantages to incorporating, including: heavier taxes; higher initial investment; and many government restrictions and reports.

NAME YOUR BUSINESS

The importance of the name of a new company cannot be overlooked, but surprisingly, it often is. The name that you give to your new business can significantly affect the business's chances of success. You must be able to distance yourself enough from what you're naming to find out how your customers perceive your business, what they want from it, and what it can do to fill the needs they believe they have. Try to be ever-conscious of your customers' demands; let the name of your company serve your customers, as well as instill confidence in them.

To begin the process, gather a pool of information concerning your company. First, describe what you are naming. What services will your business provide? Whom do you want your name to appeal to? Make a list of the names that you like and dislike. Use this list as a reference guide, and explain what appeals to you about your favorites, and what repels you from liking other names. Write down your competitors' names, and see where they fit onto your list. Can your business's name compete with others'?

After you have gathered some pertinent information, then you can start toying with some ideas for the name of your business. Keep in mind that there are still many things to consider when naming a company that you might not ordinarily have contemplated. Here are five hints which concern the naming of a new company:

1. Avoid initials. A company name like AAA WEDDING CONSULTANTS lacks personality and is easily ignored by potential customers.

2. Avoid names that resemble the names of larger corporations. For example, if your name is Harold R. Block and you happen to run a tax preparation service, calling your business H.R. Block Tax Preparation might bring a stern letter from the lawyers of H&R Block—even though you're only using your own name.

3. Avoid the timeworn and hackneyed word "Enterprises." Look in any telephone directory and you will discover hundreds of firms with names like DOE ENTERPRISES or JD ENTERPRISES. It's outmoded and rather amateurish.

4. Avoid using your family name in the name of the firm. A family name usually implies smallness, and even though you *are* a home-based business it may not be in the best interest of your image to broadcast that fact. There are many exceptions to this rule, but it is still usually sound advice.

5. Give a sense of balance and rhythm to the name of your company. Avoid long-winded, obscure, or complicated names.

Selecting a name is a very personal and creative activity; you are the one who has to live with the name you choose. It's your money that will promote it and build its reputation, and it's your name that will be associated with it. A solid name can help give you a head start. A clever name is a form of free advertising. A stodgy name will forever be a hindrance to your success.

REGISTER YOUR NAME

The purpose of registering your name is threefold:

1. To record your name so no one else can use it.
2. So you will receive mail addressed to your company's address or post office box.
3. So you will be able to cash checks made out to your company name.

Before you go to your county clerk's office to register your name, however, you must decide whether you will use your home address or a post office box. This decision is especially important if you will be offering your service primarily or exclusively by mail order.

Another option is to include both your street address *and* a P.O. box number; in fact, in some states, if you are using a P.O. box, you are *required* to also list your street address. Your street address and P.O. box must be within the same ZIP code. When you list your address like this —

Acme Typing Service
133 Colonial Street
P.O. Box 1234
Anderson, IL 55555

—the mail will be delivered to the P.O. box, yet the customer still has the "visual image" of your solid street address.

If you've decided to use a P.O. box, the annual fee is currently about $30. You will be given a box number and two keys (or a combination). If no boxes are currently available, you will be placed on a waiting list.

With your company name in mind and your mailing address, you are now ready to go to your county clerk's office to register them. You must file a fictitious name certificate if you are using a name other than your own. Even if your name is Jack Wilson and your company name is Wilson's Typing Service, that is a fictitious name. Only if you were operating under the name Jack Wilson would you be exempt from this step.

The county clerk has a file of all the business trade names in the county, arranged alphabetically either in an index card file or on computer. Call or visit the county clerk's office and tell them you want to register a new business name. They will direct you to the file containing current business names. (Some offices will conduct the search for you.) You simply look in the file to see if there is a business which is currently operating under the name you have chosen. If there is, go to your second choice for a name, and so on. If there are none, you are in luck and you can proceed. The search should take you about fifteen minutes or less. Some offices will conduct the search for you, especially if it's on computer.

The next step is to fill out a few short forms provided by the county clerk. Get the forms notarized (there is often a notary public on the premises), pay the county clerk the registration fee, which ranges from $10 to $100, and you're done. Be sure to get three copies of the forms; you'll need one to open a bank account, one for the state tax department, and one for your own records.

In some cases, the above step can be conducted entirely by mail. The county clerk will send you the forms to complete and have notarized, and you return the form with payment so the office can do the search. They'll inform you if the name you have chosen is already in use.

Open a Bank Account

If you have a good, longstanding relationship with a particular bank—one at which you have your personal checking account or savings account, for instance—that is where you should go to open a checking account for your business. Tell one of the bank officers of your intentions. He or she will have you fill out a few conventional forms, will take your new business name and mailing address for the checks and deposit slips, and will also take a small deposit to open the account.

Inform the State

For the purposes of remitting sales tax which you collect from your customers, you must file some forms with your state's Department of Taxation and Finance. Write or call them to obtain the form. Fill out the simple form they send, return it, and within a few weeks you will receive a validated Certificate of Authority which allows you to collect sales taxes. The Certificate's I.D. number will typically be your Social Security number. This costs you nothing.

Other Legalities

The FTC rule. If you're selling your product or service via mail order, the only federal department that has jurisdiction over elements of mail order is the Federal Trade Commission (FTC). If your business will be receiving orders from out of your state—which it most certainly will—the FTC requires that you abide by its Mail Order Rule. It states that unless you clearly specify in your ads or catalogs that merchandise will be shipped within a certain frame of time ("allow four to six weeks for delivery"), you must ship the order within thirty days of your receipt of the order. Failure to comply with this rule could result in stiff penalties. You can obtain a copy of the rule and other information by writing to: The Federal Trade Commission, Pennsylvania Avenue at 6th Street N.W., Washington, D.C. 20580.

Zoning. Although zoning is rarely a problem for the small operator, you should check with your county about zoning ordinances. They vary from state to state, and sometimes from county to county. If your business begins to get large, and you're still operating out of your home, large shipments of packages to and from your home may not be tolerated by your zoning laws (or your neighbors). Check it out.

Special rules. Be aware that some states, such as Wisconsin, have special rules for running a mail order operation. Check with your state authorities to be sure you are in compliance with all laws.

Insurance

Does the owner of a home business need business insurance? Yes! Regardless of the size of your business, proper coverage is essential for survival. The value of your operation must be shielded from unexpected calamities. It's difficult to think how a typing service could possibly harm one of your customers, but if someone gets sick through your lunch service, you could have a lawsuit on your hands. Your property's value must be made safe from both the "Acts of God" and man.

Loss of property. Some losses are defined as "Acts of God," such as lightning striking your home office. These are what the law "blames" on God. You can't sue Him, obviously, but you can collect from an insurer if you have property coverage. Equally costly losses are the acts of man: arson, vandalism, bombing, malicious mischief, riot, theft, or the negligent act of an employee or stranger. You will most likely be able to punish the wrong-doer and collect your loss by legal means.

Proper value protection. A business, no matter how affluent, cannot afford to cover all of its values and risks against all kinds of losses. You'd be "insurance poor" if you tried. Therefore, when you lose some or much of these dollar values, they must be replaced. The best replacer is a proper protection plan equal to the maximum potential loss.

Your plan. Business property and casualty insurance consists of coverage for property values and liability exposures. Broad property coverage is available in many states. It insures real and personal values. All-risk coverage (subject to reasonable exclusions) is better than less costly named perils protection. If it's available in your state, ask for replacement cost instead of actual cash value coverage to recover the greatest amount of your loss.

It's important to buy the biggest deductibles you can

afford so you can buy big amounts of protection for the same dollars. Ask your agent to explain the co-insurance clause in a property policy.

About your lawsuit policy: Since needs vary by size and type of business, it is not possible to make specific recommendations. Your agent may say that the market for certain kinds of liability protection is tight, so insist that he gets the broadest form in the largest amount with a deductible you can handle. Embellish that plan with an umbrella policy, one that picks up where the other policy leaves off.

How much insurance? What you buy should be determined by what a survey of your business shows. Even if yours is a new operation in your home or garage, ask for an insurance survey. The company writing your homeowner's policy may agree to write a separate policy on the business property and to extend your homeowners policy's liability portion, for a charge, to the business activities.

Ask if your present auto policy now covers business use of cars. If not, have your agent help you to accommodate your policy to fit these specifications.

SET UP YOUR OFFICE

You're registered and ready to go. Now it's time to set up the office for your computer service. The descriptions of the specific businesses in Parts Four, Five, and Six will state what equipment you will need, if any, for those businesses. Here we'll cover what you might need in the way of stationery and basic office supplies.

Business Stationery

You may find this hard to believe, but many firms may refuse to do business with you unless you use business stationery. One wholesale supplier relates that he was flooded with orders from one novice which were scribbled on bits and pieces of paper. The addresses were illegible, orders were sent to the wrong people, and complaints began to pour in. After that experience, the wholesaler absolutely refused to do business with any beginners.

You must present a professional image from the start, and this is most easily done with professional-looking stationery—letterhead and envelopes. It's important for contacting suppliers, distributors, wholesalers, and drop shippers, for sending press releases to the media, and for correspondence with customers. It's well worth the small cost and extra effort.

To start you off, you will typically need 500 sheets of letterhead paper, 500 envelopes, and 1,000 business cards imprinted with your name, business name, address, and phone number.

Miscellaneous office supplies include: a rubber stamp for imprinting your company name and address; an endorsement stamp for all of those checks that will be coming in; a binder for holding your sales tax records; and a desk-sized stapler. You most likely have most of these things around the house already, and if you don't, don't go out and spend a lot of money on all of it. Buy what you need as you need it.

Don't be tempted to buy fancy gadgets or expensive machines. Put your cash to better use in promotion and advertising.

The only other requirements are a desk, a small file cabinet, and a small room or a quiet corner in your house or apartment in which to work. You may also need a bookshelf for trade magazines and books.

Part Two:

CREATE A BUSINESS PLAN

WRITE YOUR BUSINESS PLAN

Even though you will be operating your business at home, don't take it lightly. If you expect it to succeed and grow, you need an overall plan of action. You begin by creating your business plan. Many businesses—large and small—fail because they had no plan. Properly completed, a business plan will provide the guidance needed to handle routine business details, as well as the business's direction for the future. One caution about business plans must be emphasized: the successful business plan must be developed from an unemotional, objective viewpoint, and the more complete it is, the greater the chance you will have of succeeding in your new business. The purposes of a business plan are described below.

Objective Analysis

The complete business plan is the result of a careful and thorough thought process. It answers common questions before the answers are needed. Your plan should tell you what the next step is. Finances will be accounted for, and records will support your quest for expansion financing. Most importantly your business goals will be achieved.

- *Your business.* The business plan begins with a clear, concise description of your business objectives. Essentially, it is a statement defining how you are going to make money. This portion of the plan should be succinct, but complete enough so that anyone reading it will know what you intend to do, and why it is likely to succeed.

- *Your markets.* How does your business fill a need in the market? What is the size of the total market? What is likely to be your share of that market, and how was this determined? What is unique about your product or service that gives it an edge in the market?

- *Your competition.* Do you have any competition, and how will that affect your business? What advantages do you have over the competition in your market? What advantages does the competition have, and how will you offset these advantages? If other companies have entered this market, why have they succeeded or failed?

- *Your location.* Does location of your home play a role in the success of your business? Will operating the business from home be a detriment to the business? If so, how will you deal with that?

- *Your management.* Who will manage your business? If more than one person is involved, how will duties and responsibilities be divided? Who makes the final decision when required? What outside services, such as accounting, legal services, or marketing consultants, will be needed to assist management?

- *Use of funds.* If you need outside start-up funds—from a bank or a relative—your source of financial support will want a detailed plan of how the money will be used. This will require a breakdown of equipment, salaries, rents, utilities, raw materials, and advertising.

Financial Information

Financial data is important for more than just obtaining a loan. It is part of your objective analysis. It will determine how much business you must conduct in order to make an acceptable profit. It will identify expenses that might have been overlooked, or make it clear that equipment and services that you initially thought were essential will have to be postponed. An important function of the financial planning is that it gives you a standard by which to measure your success. Comparing expenses, income, and profits to the plan will quickly allow you to identify success, or the need to overhaul the plan. Some essential parts of the financial portion of the business plan are:

Financial sources. Financial sources refer not only to banks and investors, but also to your personal bank account.

Equipment list. Do you have the necessary equipment to carry your business through the initial stages of your plan, and if not, what will be needed? Note that "essential" is the operative word, and is not the same as "ideal." Obtain only the equipment necessary to accomplish the initial goals of your business plan.

Balance sheet. Complete a balance sheet showing assets and liabilities. You will probably be surprised at your own net worth. Properly completed, the balance sheet will show your success and prevent early financial disasters, if maintained on a regular basis.

Break-even analysis. Compare the cost of doing business with the gross receipts. There should be money left over after expenses—including your salary—are accounted for, or you are not making a profit.

Cash-flow analysis. On a month-by-month basis for at least a three-year period, determine all expenses, both known and projected, as well as all income that is projected. After two to three years, there should be a steady increase in the profits. The business plan is a living document. It should be consulted frequently to ensure that your business plan stays on track. It should also be reviewed and revised as necessary on a regular basis. A business plan can be three pages or 300 pages. It is not the length that counts, but the thought that goes into it. In the world of fast-paced business, the only truly winning business plan is the one that raises financing without collateral. It sells you and your business. It shows that you have the ability and understanding to make your business work. It also provides a clear road map to success, and this is an important function of the business plan, even if you do not seek venture capital, partnerships, or bank financing. If you have answered all of the questions above, the only question left unanswered now is how soon will it succeed.

HOW MUCH MONEY WILL YOU NEED?

The charts on the following pages will help you estimate how much money you'll need to start your home business. Fill them in according to your particular circumstances. If you already have a typewriter, for example, you needn't fill in the cost for that item. Fill in only the costs of items you will have to purchase.

Regarding the chart of estimated monthly expenses, the basic estimated monthly cost for each item depends on the size of your anticipated operation. You can best derive these estimates on what you reasonably expect in annual sales. Note that after each monthly estimate a number indicates whether you should double, triple, or quadruple the monthly figure to arrive at an allocation for a start-up period (which averages three months). These are factors suggested by the Small Business Administration.

COST OF SETTING UP YOUR OFFICE

Use the following checklist to lay out your own cost estimates of various aspects of setting up your business, including start-up costs. These are one-time expenses. Add other necessary items.

Furniture, Fixtures, Equipment:
    Special equipment for the business $_____
    _____ $_____
    _____ $_____
    Typewriter $_____
    Storage shelves $_____
    Desk and chair $_____
    File cabinet $_____
    Safe or strongbox $_____
    Other furniture, fixtures, equipment $_____
Decorating and remodeling costs:
    Starting inventory $_____
    Deposits with public utilities $_____
    Legal and other professional fees $_____
    Licenses and permits $_____
    Advertising and promotion for
        opening $_____
    Accounts receivable (money for
        stock until credit customers pay) $_____
    Cash (for unexpected expenses,
        losses, special unforeseen
        purchases, etc.) $_____

Total estimated cash needed to set up office and
    start business $_____

ESTIMATED MONTHLY EXPENSES

The following checklist shows typical items on a cost-of-operation breakdown. Base your monthly estimate on expected annual sales, then multiply by the indicated *factor* to derive an estimate of the amount you will need, as start-up, for each item. Do not hesitate to alter any given factor if there is good reason to do so. Add other items that may be relevant to your business.

	Monthly Cost Estimate		Start-Up Cost Estimate
Salary of owner-manager	$_____	x2	$_____
All other salaries and wages	$_____	x3	$_____
Rent, if any	$_____	x3	$_____
Promotion and advertising	$_____	x3	$_____
Delivery expenses	$_____	x3	$_____
Telephone and fax	$_____	x3	$_____
Other utilities	$_____	x3	$_____
Insurance	$_____	*	$_____
Taxes, including Social Security	$_____	x4	$_____
Interest	$_____	x3	$_____
Maintenance	$_____	x3	$_____
Legal, other professional fees	$_____	x3	$_____
Miscellaneous	$_____	x3	$_____

Total estimated cash needed at start for operational costs $_____

*Payment as required by insurance company.

FINDING START-UP FUNDS

Most home businesses can be started with one's own funds. But some are more expensive to begin than others. For a mobile disk jockey service, for example, you may need extra start-up funding to purchase the necessary stereo equipment and music. If so, don't borrow more than you really need. If you lack the business experience to arrive at a reliable estimate of your financial need (see the previous charts), seek advice from the SBA. Once you have a firm idea about the amount of capital you must acquire, you can better decide where to look.

Check Your Own Resources

Surprisingly, many people seem to be blind to the amount of collateral they have. Perhaps you have invested several thousand dollars in CDs or Savings Bonds over the years, or maybe you own some stock of value. If so, don't rush out to cash them; use them as collateral to obtain a loan from your bank or some other lending institution. You may also have an insurance policy having a cash value against which you can float an alternative or additional loan. Do you own the house in which you live? If so, you may have money-getting equity. And what about your car? If you own it free and clear, and it is fairly new and in good condition, it may be good as collateral for a few more bucks. But bear this in mind: if you need a different kind of car for your new business—perhaps a mini-van with which to transport equipment and supplies—it might be a good idea to trade the old car in for a new one that will serve both personal and business needs, and only then seek a loan using the car as collateral (provided that you don't buy the new one on installment).

If You Need a Friend

Perhaps you have a friend or a relative who has some extra money tucked away in a savings account, or who owns property that could be used as collateral for a loan. If your business idea is sound, he or she may be more than willing to serve as a financial backer. Don't expect friends or relatives to help you unless you offer something in return to compensate them for the risk they are taking. Your counter offer may involve nothing more complicated than the written promise to pay them a higher interest rate than they can earn at a bank.

Part Three:

MARKET YOUR
SERVICE

Marketing is the most important element of any business because it is all about how to *stay* in business once you've started it. The only way you can make money with whatever business you choose is to: (a) let the public know your service is available; and then (b) persuade them to call your service instead of someone else's. This you do through advertising, promotion, and other forms of marketing.

At this stage in the process, you should have already done your market survey, and found out what equipment and supplies you'll need. Maybe you've already got some customers lined up for your service. But you want to get repeat business, and you want your satisfied customers to refer you to additional customers. That takes visibility and credibility, and that's where your marketing efforts come in.

There are several ways to tell your business story to the community: (1) through "free" advertising in the form of publicity; (2) by taking print ads in local media; (3) through direct mail solicitation and handbill distribution; (4) by running special promotions. First, however, the matter of your credibility must be addressed, and to solve that problem you must create a professional image.

CREATE A PROFESSIONAL IMAGE

No matter how hard you work or how in-demand your service is, if you do not convey a professional image to potential customers you are setting yourself up for failure. The home business operator who has his five-year-old answer the phone, and uses an off-center rubber stamp to create stationery will have a difficult time projecting an air of professionalism.

There are three vital steps you should take right now if you want to conduct business in a manner that will inspire confidence:

1. *Create a home office.* A home office—a real office in your home set apart from the family room, screaming children, the blare of TVs and stereos, and kitchen noises—can help you to create the appropriate atmosphere in which to conduct your business—even if you never have to invite a client in. Keeping your business materials all in one place will help you protect the continuity of your work.

   If you do not have a spare bedroom or den to use as a home office, you will have to use your imagination. Consider converting your garage, basement, laundry room, walk-in closet, an alcove, or breakfast nook. If all else fails, a corner of your bedroom or living room can be converted into an office with dividers and free-standing shelves. Choose a place that is out of the mainstream of your household, that makes you feel good, one in which you will look forward to working. Wherever it is, make it pleasant. If you will be having clients or visitors, try to choose a location that is close to an entrance.

   You will gain respect, self-confidence, and the opportunity to work more efficiently when you separate the place where you work from the rest of your home.

2. *Install a separate telephone line.* The most important reason for a separate phone line is this: when the phone rings, you know it's a business call. This simple bit of information has many implications. When you answer your business line, you will always use your name or the name of your business which will give you instant credibility. You will have control over who answers the phone and what is said to the caller. For times when you do not want to take business calls, you can install a good quality answering machine or use an answering service.

Your own business line will help further separate your business from your personal life. Your answering machine can insulate your clients from inevitable household disturbances. If the baby is screaming or the dog is barking at the mailman, you can turn on your answering machine and your business phone will be answered in a calm, professional manner.

When your business has its own phone, you will be entitled to a listing in the *Yellow Pages*, and a larger advertisement if you want to pay the additional costs. These are excellent ways to obtain new clients.

3. *Use carefully designed printed materials.* Your business cards, stationery, brochures—all of your printed materials represent you and your business. Quality paper that feels good to the touch combined with an appealing typeface and an exclusive logo will give the recipient an

unspoken message. The first impression that your mailing makes will determine whether or not it is read.

Even though a new business can be short on funds, you cannot afford to skimp on printed materials. Hire a professional artist to design a logo and graphic image for your business. All of your promotional materials should be typeset (or at least done on a good laser printer), and your correspondence should be typed on an office-quality typewriter or printer. Your printed material represents you in the minds of your clients. If you want your business to have instant recognition, create a communications package that will help you convey your professionalism.

Even more than a traditional office-based business, the business operating out of a home must be careful of the image it projects.

HOW TO GET "FREE" PUBLICITY

Public relations (PR) is a highly specialized, sometimes expensive area of marketing. If you paid a PR firm to get stories about your business published in local newspapers and magazines, you would probably wonder just what is meant by "free" publicity. Fortunately, in a small business like yours, it should be a fairly simple matter to become your own press agent. A few simple PR techniques will go a long way toward gaining visibility for your service at a fraction of the cost of conventional advertising.

The first thing you need to do is generate a local-area media list. Get the names of editors of local newspapers, shopper papers, and magazines. Do the same thing with feature editors of local television stations, as well as with hosts of local talk radio and cable TV programs. About two weeks before you formally open for business, notify these people that you're open for business. The most professional way to do this is with a simple press kit, which for this kind of business might contain the following elements:

- A press release that announces the opening of your business, describes what your business does, your hours of operation, your availability, your professionalism, your enthusiasm, etc.

- Photograph of you, the owner, posed at your place of business or actually "performing" your service.

- A one-page press release "bio" that covers something about your background, your enterprising hopes and dreams, and why you started the business.

- A one-paragraph cover letter.

Also include your business card in the press kit for ease of reference. Put the whole package into a simple pocket folder, and send it out first class. You only have to send your "grand opening" press kit to the media one time, although from time to time you may be asked to send the whole package. If this happens some time after you have opened for business, you will want to substitute the "now-open-for-business" announcement for a more current press release. Perhaps you've given a big donation to the United Way, or perhaps you're celebrating your business anniversary. Such newsworthy items will be the lead for the current press release, which you will include in your updated press kit.

Subsequent press releases will usually not include a fancy press-kit pocket folder. Instead, they will consist of the one- or two-page release, business card, and photograph. Generally, you'll have a better chance of getting a story printed if you include photographs; the media like the show-and-tell approach, even if they decide not to run a photo. The photographs themselves should be black-and-white glossy prints or color slides or transparencies. It's best not to send color prints because they are the hardest to duplicate in the printing process.

Some people go all out in their press kits and include something extra in them. If you have the money, you might want to send out an *advertising specialty* of some kind, such as a key chain or an eraser that is imprinted with your company name, phone number, and logo. Advertising specialty companies are listed in the *Yellow Pages*, and salespeople will work with you to choose the item that is most suited to your business. Although this is an extra expense, it is something that you can use as an advertising gimmick for a long period of time. You might want to leave one of your ad specialties with each new client, as a reminder to call for service again.

WRITE A PRESS RELEASE

Local and metro newspapers have discovered that their readers are quite interested in the business activities of persons in their community. Frequently they publish feature stories of local-area businesses. There is no guarantee that a story about your business will get picked up by any publication. To make sure your press material gets top consideration, send out the most professional package you can. In addition to the guidelines above, the following points should help you get coverage:

- Make your copy informative and as interesting as possible, concentrating on any newsworthy details.

- Keep it short and concise; two paragraphs is about the right length.

- The copy must be neatly typed, error-free, and double-spaced with wide margins.

- On the top left-hand side of the page, be sure to type: FOR IMMEDIATE RELEASE. Underneath that, type the date.

- If you send out your release to a number of media sources, have it professionally photocopied.

- Be sure the release includes all pertinent information, such as the company name and address, plus hours of operation or availability.

- Hire a good photographer to shoot whatever pictures you include with the press kit or with subsequent press releases. Most cities have at least one such photo service. Use the *Yellow Pages* and check around for the best prices. The prints should be glossy, of high contrast, and a minimum of 4" x 5" in size. Business owners who have a media list of several hundred names sometimes keep costs down by ordering four 4" x 5"s printed on a single 8" x 10" sheet, and cutting them later.

- Make yourself available to the media for follow-up questions and explanations. Be prepared to talk about the range of services you offer and any "tips" for readers or viewers on some aspect of your operation or related problems. You should be enthusiastic about the service you're providing.

The release should go out to as many publications as you can afford. Because your service will most likely be concentrated in the local area (although you might be able to market it via mail order, too), this should be no problem for you.

Some people are nervous about writing a press release for the first time. The first step is to look carefully through the newspapers and pick out stories about local businesses. Notice how many of these stories have pictures with them. Collect these stories and photographs over a period of several weeks; you can do this while you're lining up suppliers and other materials for your business. Put these stories in a folder and set them aside for the time being. Now you're ready to assemble your press kit and move on to step two. Take the time to read through the stories about local businesses, and you will find that they present information in pretty much the same way. In fact, you can almost fill in the blanks, from one business to another. Why is this so? Because most of these stories were developed from press kits that were provided by the business owners themselves! Now all you have to do is follow the format of existing stories, adapting the language to fit your particular business.

FROM DIRECT MAIL TO DIRECT CONTACT

Advertising experts agree that you should explore every aspect of free or nearly free forms of publicity, described above, before you spend one dime on advertising. But your home business may not lend itself to free press coverage on a regular basis. That's why you'll have to put a more formal advertising program in place. Direct mail is one good way of targeting client prospects in this business.

In direct mail, you send out information about your service in the form of a sales letter, brochure, coupon, or handbill—or any combination thereof. You send these mailings to the names of people on a mailing list. Where do you get this list? Either you compile a list of people who have already used your service, or you rent a mailing list. If you're just starting out, you do not yet have a customer list. So you can rent a list from a list broker.

Be forewarned, however: Direct mail may not be a good idea for the beginner on a budget. For one thing, unless you are just sending out inexpensive flyers, it can be quite expensive. First you must buy or rent a list from a qualified broker, then create an attractive, effective mailing piece, and then pay for envelopes and postage. And remember that you can only expect a 2 to 3 percent response rate from such a mailing, even if you confine your mailing to a local neighborhood area.

If you are focusing on the household market, you can rent lists of homeowners and apartment dwellers in specific ZIP codes—sometimes specific neighborhoods within ZIP codes. But because of the costs involved, it is probably best to wait until you have compiled your own list of customers (from sales through newspaper and magazine ads), then periodically send them brochures or handbills that describe your service.

You can rent mailing lists of businesses in specific ZIP codes or industry segments. Again, there are significant minimum costs involved with identifying and targeting the persons who may be in charge of negotiating with services such as yours. On the other hand, you can save money if you start following the new-business listings in your area. You can make a practice of compiling names and addresses of businesspeople to contact as you build your business. When it's time to start marketing your service, you will have a list all ready for mailing.

Once you have a track record, you might want to give direct mail a shot, particularly if you are expanding the scope of your business to include a variety of services beyond your original idea. As we've stated, with the right list, a well-done direct mail package to the right customer list can be quite effective in bringing in new service orders.

Where to Get Mailing Lists

You can find mailing list brokers by looking in your nearest big city *Yellow Pages* under "Advertising—Direct Mail" or "Mailing Lists." A good broker will have access to mailing lists for every possible category of client: homeowner, apartment dweller, apartment managers, plumbing contractors, dentists. Some list names are printed on self-adhesive labels, while others come on computer disks and can be slipped into your PC. Rental prices vary accordingly. Some lists include telephone numbers, and others do not. When you rent a list, you are authorized to use that list only once.

The Direct Mail Piece

Above all, a direct mail piece must be interesting. This

is true whether you're sending out a one-page handbill or a five-piece mailing package. Many times, self-mailers (a direct mail piece that is folded and stamped to form its own envelope) or ordinary envelopes addressed to "Resident" look like junk mail for recipients to throw away unopened and unread. If you use self-mailers, therefore, you need to have a "hook" that will persuade the recipient to open and read the material that's inside.

Here are some ways to get the most out of direct mail:

- Enclose reprints of your display ads or articles written about your company.
- Encourage service orders with discount offers.
- Include a deadline notice, such as "Call before May 15."

A self-mailer measuring 8½" x 11" can be printed and trifolded by an offset printing house. Use either card stock or 20-lb. colored paper stock. What's inside the mailer can take many forms: an information piece that announces the availability of your service, a dollars-off coupon, or the equivalent of a big display ad or a handbill. The purpose of the self-mailer is quite simple: to motivate the recipient to call you and place a service order. A self-mailer can also save money on postage.

Using Brochures, Handbills, Coupon Mailers

You will need to have on hand a standard informational brochure that describes the services you offer. The pitch letters you send out to customer prospects will change on a regular basis, and you can have special handbills or coupons printed as they are required. Have an offset printer run 2,000 or so copies of a brochure (trifolded 8½" x 11" or single-folded 7¼" x 8½") that highlights all the services you provide. A little-known way to heighten impact is to use a gray or light blue card stock and an ink like navy or dark magenta. This should cost about the same as boring old black ink and white card stock, but it will be perceived as a professional, two-color piece.

For an initial mailing to commercial clients, write an enthusiastic, one-page pitch letter that introduces your service and asks for business. Mail the letter, brochure, and your business card in a standard #10 envelope to your list of names. After you have been in business for a while, redo your pitch letter in the form of a reminder that you offer competitive services to the business community. You should also develop a standard pitch letter that you send out to new businesses in the community, in which you make the new enterprise aware of your services. A colorful first class commemorative stamp often improves response rate. If business prospects don't call you, follow up by phone about ten days later to remind them of who you are and what you offer.

Handbills are sometimes considered to be the same as brochures, but the term usually refers to single sheets of paper handed out to passersby or placed on car windshields. Some handbills are produced in the form of door-hangers that are put on doorknobs. Typically, they are inexpensive to produce in large volume at an offset house.

A good handbill has all the features of good direct mail or ad copy, and it may be used to announce everything from a grand opening to a discount promotion. The expensive aspect of handbills is distribution, for you're going to have to pay somebody to put handbills on the windshield or doorknob of every car or front door in a neighborhood. If you can't find some students to distribute your handbills in a neighborhood after school, you might ask your offset printer to refer you to people who distribute handbills for a living.

Another way to distribute handbills is to put them up as notices on community bulletin boards. Often, such boards have restrictions about the kinds of notices that can be placed on them. If you're only allowed to post index cards on a board, then it's worth the effort to get your promotional information printed on some colored index cards. You can place these on boards, automobiles, and front doors, or you can hand them out to customers and ask them to pass the information along to their friends. This can be an effective way of improving word-of-mouth advertising.

Coupon mailers have become popular in many cities in recent years. Coupon-mail advertising, sometimes called cooperative direct mail advertising, is an offshoot of more conventional direct mail advertising. A typical cooperative direct mail package is not personalized but is sent to "Resident" or "Occupant" in a localized market area. It usually includes discount offers from a dozen or so noncompeting local advertisers. Coupons from one car wash, one pizza parlor, one maid service, and so on, will be included in the package. A coupon mailer, which may be one-, two-, or (sometimes) four-color, generally measures $3\frac{5}{8}$" x $8\frac{1}{2}$" and fits perfectly into a #10 envelope. Costs for the advertiser are roughly competitive with display advertising.

HOW TO USE CLASSIFIED AND DISPLAY ADS

As a beginner, you may be unsure whether you should begin with an inexpensive classified ad, or take a chance on a more eye-catching display ad. There are reasons for using one or the other.

You use classified ads:

1. When you want to receive inquiries from potential customers, then follow up those inquiries with literature to close the sale.
2. To sell directly from the ad, to persons who are "presold" and who simply want to order a particular service.

You use a display ad:

1. When you want to use a photo, logo, or other illustration to project the professionalism and strong image of your company.
2. When you want to attract attention to your company and receive service-order calls.
3. When your service appeals to a large segment of the target market.
4. When you need the space to tell the complete story of your company's concept.

Classified Ads

Classified advertising is generally recognized as the least expensive way to get news of your service's availability before the market. Virtually all magazines and newspapers that you will be using carry a classified section, and in most communities there will be at least two publications that will be available to sustain an ad campaign. Aside from being low in cost, a classified ad is the easiest to get into print and an inexpensive way to get a great deal of experience in telling your story in the least number of words possible.

You doubtless know what a classified ad looks like; in this trade it is a short-worded message containing a direct, brief statement or "pitch," and a telephone number. Classified ads are published in local bulletins, community newspapers, shopper papers, weekly and daily newspapers, and a variety of magazines.

The price of a classified ad is usually determined by the number of words it contains. Some newspapers with small circulations charge by the line. The large publications that charge on a per-word basis charge anywhere from $1 to $7—or more—per word. The larger the publication's circulation (number of readers), the higher the per-word price. In a local paper with a circulation of 30,000 readers, for example, the word rate would be in the neighborhood of 25¢ to 55¢. This low rate is due to the relative "overhead" costs of keeping that publication alive. In a magazine with a circulation of 300,000 (such as a glossy "city" magazine), word rates may range from $2 to $5 per word.

Placing the Ad

Place your ad in the area publications which your target clients are most likely to read. Since you will probably be charged by the word, you will have to learn to write concisely, making every word work hard for the money you are spending. Your name and telephone number will probably amount to four words, so the body copy of your ad will probably consist of another ten to fifteen words. The best classified ads never go beyond twenty words. As an example, here is an ad you might place for a tax preparation service:

> APRIL 15 IS COMING—Don't let the IRS take more than its fair share. Get the most deductions allowed by law. Fast, accurate, affordable tax preparation. Call Arthur, 555-5555.

To succeed with a classified ad, you must first gain the attention of the reader. The appeal of your service should be one of four things: what the reader wants to *gain, save, do,* or *be.* The most successful ads lead off by promising to *do* something of benefit to the reader, or to make him want to *gain* more information. This selling technique also applies to display advertising, as we shall see. Experiment with ways to incorporate some informational sale copy into your classified ad. The idea in the above ad is to motivate readers to telephone you. Every name you generate from an ad is one that you can add to your house file. You can either arrange an appointment to submit a proposal over the phone or send the prospect a brochure and then follow up a week later.

Display Ads

Display ads, like classified ads, will be geared toward publications such as newspapers and magazines, and you will undoubtedly find that once you start placing classified ads, the advertising sales departments of various publications will be encouraging you to "trade up" to display advertising. There is even a hybrid form of print advertising known as the "classified display ad." This kind of ad, which is quite common in glossy city magazines, usually includes standard classified copy, plus a simple piece of art such as a logo. But display ads and even classified display ads are not confined to periodicals. The *Yellow Pages*, local TV guides that are available at supermarket checkout counters, and cooperative coupon mailers are all potential outlets for your display advertising efforts. You might find yourself adapting a basic display ad to the needs of a particular medium. As you gain experience in advertising, you will see what alterations in your basic message have to be made.

What is the secret to successful display advertising? It's really no secret at all. All it takes are three things:

1. You've got to offer a service that people want, or at least *think* they want.

2. You've got to know when and where to advertise your service—which magazine or directory to use, which month or day to run your ad.

3. Your ad must motivate people to action.

So far, we've shown you how to achieve or find numbers one and two. Now on to number three.

How to Write Good Ads

First, let us define what we mean by a "good ad." The

criterion for a good ad is clear cut. An ad that produces a profit, either by pulling service orders directly, or by getting inquiries that are converted into sales through follow-up literature is a good ad. Results can be measured right down to the last penny, and the results are what count.

Your ad will be competing with dozens of others to attract the attention of the reader. Unless you can get the reader at least to glance at your ad, by attracting his or her attention, your service can be the best within a hundred miles, but you won't sell anything.

Imagine yourself on a railroad track with an express train speeding toward you. You want to tell the engineer that the bridge up ahead is washed out. First you've got to get him to stop. Somehow you must attract his attention. Only after he stops the train can you tell him about the bridge. You pick up a small red flag and begin waving it desperately. Your most eloquent and persuasive description of the bridge is useless unless the engineer stops the train and listens to what you say.

Attract Attention

Your reader is the engineer of the train. He's glancing over the dozens of ads quickly. His eye catches a headline or a picture. He slows the train momentarily, then resumes speed. Now he's coming at your ad. The headline of your ad is your "flag."

So much for the analogy. So how do you attract attention in a display ad? As you will see, there are essentially four basic ways. Each will be discussed in detail:

1. The "angle."

2. The headline.

3. The picture.

4. The layout.

The "Angle"

What is your basic advertising appeal? This is your angle. In short, your angle is what your service can do for your customer. Your prospect has a one-track mind. His or her motivation for buying any service is self-interest. He or she asks one question: "Why would I want to use this service?" Answer this question. Show in words and/or pictures how your service can provide what the customer desires.

Customers want: comfort, convenience; more leisure time; good service; security; new ways of doing things; bargains; enjoyment.

They want to improve their: appearance; self-confidence; personality; status; personal prestige.

Notice that not one of the above qualities has anything specific to do with any particular business. Although you are *selling* a specific service, customers are *buying* convenience, comfort, security, leisure, and status. Sell them the basics—what they need.

The Headline

Use as many words as it takes to attract attention and to offer the angle. Strictly speaking, there is no limit to the number of words in a good headline, although many advertisers have found that the fewer words it takes to attract attention, the better. More important, there *are* key words that can often increase the power of a headline tremendously. Here is a partial list:

absolutely	easy	latest	secret
amazing	exciting	lifetime	sensational
approved	exclusive	lowest	simplified
authentic	fortune	magic	special
bargain	free	miracle	strong
better	genuine	powerful	surprise
complete	gift	profitable	tested
confidential	guaranteed	quality	unique
delivered	improved	rare	valuable
discount	largest	revolutionary	wealth

You may think these words are overworked and lack punch. But repeated tests prove that they out-pull clever, intellectual words by a wide margin.

In a headline, there is probably no word that attracts more attention and public interest than the word "FREE." No other word in the language can do more for your ad. If you can find a way to offer something for free, by all means do so. Consider, for example, offering some free tutoring to a customer who referred your service to five other people.

The Picture

If you have room, use a logo or some other picture that evokes what your service does to help tell your story. Many services that take large *Yellow Pages* ads simply use clip art. Whoever designs your ad, or takes your photographs, is a creative type, and may have some interesting ideas for visuals. Whatever kind of picture you decide to use, it should be easy on the eye, neither too busy nor too obscure for the reader to realize at once the kind of service he's being asked to deal with.

The Layout

On a small two-inch or three-inch display ad, there isn't much you can do about layout. You can arrange line drawings, margins, and type to match the contour of your illustrations, or use a bold border. Don't be afraid to experiment with effective ways of making your layout different from all the others. Notice what competitors do, and try to make your ads at least as exciting as theirs.

Basically, a layout will attract attention in one of two ways, if it is: (1) made dynamically powerful so it dominates the page by its visual impact; and (2) made so simple and plain that its sheer restraint, on a page filled with bold, dynamic ads, captures the reader's attention.

Body Copy

Now that you have captured the interest of your readers, you must sell them on your new service. Here's how:

1. Tell about the value and benefits of your service.

2. Prove it.

3. Persuade readers to grasp these benefits.

4. Ask for action.

Your main concern is to include as much valuable information about what your service does as you can, without writing a whole book about it. The trick is to keep your reader interested. Long columns of straight body copy discourages readers. Use subheads and bulleted lists to entice the reader. The subhead is a preview of what's to come. They excite curiosity and boost interest in the lists or other copy that follows.

If possible, run your subheads in sequence, to carry your story in "shots" from beginning to end. Change the size, color, or typeface of subheads to make them stand out from lists or body copy. Use liberal white space around them to create a dynamic, easy-to-read layout.

To write powerful copy, follow these ten basic rules:

1. Use subheads.

2. Use simple, easily understood words.

3. Use short words, short sentences, short paragraphs, but enough words to sell your readers.

4. Write copy as if you were talking to one person, not addressing an audience.

5. Use testimonials—praise from satisfied clients.

6. Include guarantees.

7. Offer a discount or money-back guarantee, if possible.

8. Tell the reader to act, and tell him why he should act *now*.

9. Offer a free gift.

10. Include contact information (such as your phone number) in every ad.

All of the factors that go into display advertising for publications can be applied to coupon-mailer advertising as well. There is one additional factor that most coupon-mailer advertisers take into account, and that is the limited-time element. One reason for sending a coupon to a prospective customer's home is to encourage him or her to take advantage of a special offer of some kind. A $10 discount is a good example, and if it is tied to a reminder that the offer expires on a certain date, so much the better. This encourages the prospect to act *now*.

Study ads for services similar to yours that appeal to you. Decide what makes you interested in them, why they drew your attention, and how they might influence you to take advantage of their services. Good copywriting comes with practice. Write some display ads for your service, and show them to relatives and friends to learn whether they are effective. Encourage these readers to be brutally honest with you—after all, your profitability is at stake. After a time, you will probably become quite good at it.

What if you can't catch on to the art of copywriting? There are two alternatives. First, you can take advantage of the help that advertising space salespeople offer. Many telephone directory salespeople and coupon-mail promoters offer free copywriting and layout assistance as a means of attracting advertisers. Experienced ad-space salespeople know the kind of copy and layout that will pull. Take advantage of such assistance, particularly if it doesn't add anything to your ad cost, *and as long as it works*. Your second alternative is to hire a professional copywriter. Copywriters may not be cheap (charging a minimum of $35 per hour in most markets), but when you consider that their experience can mean the difference between a failed ad and success, it may well be worth the price.

TAXES

We cannot stress enough the importance for any small or large business owner to be in full compliance with local laws, zoning ordinances, and to pay all taxes. There may be a temptation for the small operator, who is also earning a full-time income from a regular job, not to report his or her part-time earnings as part of his or her income. This is a big mistake. If you have registered your company name and have opened a business bank account, the IRS is almost certainly aware—or can easily learn—of your extra income. Don't be foolish. Declare any income you receive from your new business; the penalties you will suffer for not paying your taxes make it just not worth the risk.

Just as you pay income tax on what you may earn from regular employment, you must also acknowledge to the IRS how much you earned from your home business. If you are operating as a sole proprietor, this is easily done. The IRS views you and your business as one entity and are therefore taxed as one entity. There are no special taxes to pay because you own and run a business out of your home. On your income tax form, you simply combine your regular gross earnings with your *net* earnings to arrive at your "total income." The only difference is that during the year, much of your income tax has already been withheld at your regular job so that you don't have to come up with a huge amount of money come April 15. You have paid Social Security taxes, federal income taxes, and state and local taxes. But with your part-time business, *none* of your tax has been withheld and you must pay those taxes by the April 15th deadline.

The chances are that the Social Security taxes that you've paid through your regular job will cover your obligation in that department (there is a ceiling of maximum payment). But you will still have to pay federal, state, and local taxes. To lessen the burden come April, the federal government allows you to make quarterly payments during the year on what you estimate you will earn that year. That way, you won't have to pay a large chunk all at once.

If your home business is your sole income, making these quarterly payments is a must, as absolutely none of your income tax has been withheld during the year.

When you prepare your tax returns, you—or your accountant—will have to fill out a Schedule C, "Profit (or Loss) From Business or Profession." On this form you will figure your net profit or loss from your business which is added to (or subtracted from, if it's a loss) your regular income.

Deductions

Fortunately, if you are operating your business at home, you are allowed several deductions. If you use a particular room or section of your house exclusively for your home business, the percentages of utilities and rent or house depreciation you pay to maintain it, is deductible from your gross sole proprietorship income.

The key phrase that the IRS stresses here is—and they're very particular about it—"exclusive use." If, for example, you use your den as your office during the evenings, but your kids use it as a TV/play room during the day, then in the eyes of the IRS the room is not eligible for those deductions. The room must be used exclusively and regularly for your home business operation.

Other deductions you will be allowed include expenses for:

- Office supplies and equipment
- Subscriptions to professional journals
- Business use of your car or truck
- Utilities (heat and light)
- Repairs and maintenance of the office
- Percentage of rent
- Percentage of home depreciation
- Repairs and service contracts on office equipment
- Insurance for the business
- Business phone expenses
- Business-related travel

There is a limit as to how much you can deduct, however: the amount equal to the total income generated by your business, less the home expenses you could deduct even if you were not operating a home-based business. Mortgage interest, for example, is deductible whether or not you operate a home business, so you must subtract the business percentage of your home from your business's gross income. By doing this, you arrive at the maximum amount for home-related business deductions.

Consult your accountant, a tax specialist, or the IRS itself for more complete information.

Sales Tax

If your state has a sales and use tax, you as a vendor are required to collect this tax on all sales made to customers *within your state.* If your operation is based in New York State, for example, you must collect sales tax for only those sales to customers who reside in New York State. If the sale comes from any other state, you are not required to collect sales tax.

The percentage of tax varies from state to state and, within each state sometimes, from county to county. Again taking New York State as an example, if your business is based in Dutchess County, you need only collect 5¼ percent sales tax; if it is based in New York City, 8 percent sales tax must be collected.

It is very simple to collect and pay this sales tax. If you run ads which may pull orders from your own state, or you send mailings to customers or potential customers within your state, then you should include a line like the following on your order form:

"N.Y. State Residents add 5¼% Sales Tax"

To pay the taxes, you obtain the proper forms from your state's Department of Taxation and Finance. How often you must remit these taxes to the state depends on how much sales tax you collect. Most small operations will only have to make annual or quarterly payments, while larger operations are required to make monthly payments (in New York, monthly payments are for total taxable receipts of $300,000 or more).

The forms you must fill out with each payment are quite simple, but you must make payments promptly or you will be subject to a fine of $50 or more.

You will automatically receive the proper sales tax forms if you registered your company, as you should have, with your state as a vendor. When you do this, the state will return to you a stamped Certificate of Authority which must be prominently displayed at your place of business.

Regulations and laws concerning state sales tax vary from state to state, so you should contact your state's Department of Taxation and Finance for complete information.

Part Four:

12 PRODUCT-BASED HOME BUSINESSES

BOUDOIR PHOTOGRAPHY

"I don't tell a woman that she's going to look like a *Playboy* bunny," says "boudoir" photographer Judith Ryan. "I think every woman is beautiful in her own way, and I try to draw out that inner beauty in her portrait."

Three years ago, Judith Ryan opened a portrait studio in Seattle that specializes in taking photographs of women in erotic settings and poses for their husbands and boyfriends. Now she is earning a very respectable income and gaining a lot of personal satisfaction doing exactly what she wants to do. Established photographers may never have considered this particular photographic angle, but they will once they hear of Ryan's remarkable success.

A highly visible measure of Ryan's success with this approach to photography is the increasing number of boudoir photographers advertising in the same weekly newspaper that she advertises in. But she isn't worried about the competition because, so far at least, all of them are men, and she thinks that makes for a very different kind of photograph. "A lot of the male photographers try to make women look like sex kittens," she says. Ryan believes the women who come to her are looking for a different image: loving and sensual—and certainly not pornographic.

What Ryan strives for in her photographs is a timeless quality that she gets by achieving an intimate connection with the woman she is shooting. "They become really vulnerable and they open up to me," she says. "It's like a moment out of time for them, and a soft quality comes through." That kind of intimacy is difficult to achieve when the photographer is male, according to Ryan.

Women seem to prefer a woman photographer because they feel more comfortable taking off their clothes and striking erotic poses in front of another woman. "What we do is girl stuff, like pulling things out of your grandma's trunk and playing dress up when we were kids," says Ryan.

Sometimes grandma's trunk actually is in Ryan's pictures. Women frequently ask her to shoot their photographs in their own bedrooms because they want to include their furniture. One woman had a beautiful 100-year-old brass bed; another had a 200-year-old Victorian style bedroom set that was her grandmother's. "They want to personalize their photographs," Ryan says, "and I like the challenge of each new situation."

Shooting on location is a service that has really helped her build her business since it seems that some women enjoy showing off their furniture as much as their bodies. The antiques fit right in with the style of photographs that Ryan has come to be known for. "The pictures that I do, even though they are sensual, are really old-fashioned looking," she says. Half of her work is in black and white, and increasingly she is hand-coloring her prints to give them a vintage look.

Even though a woman may choose to come into the studio for her portrait session, Ryan asks that she bring her own props from home to use in the pictures. For some women this is a special piece of lingerie, special hat, or a flower for their hair. Others bring articles of clothing drawn from their lover's closet, such as a necktie, a man's hat, or a T-shirt. "A man's plain white T-shirt can be very erotic," Ryan says. Recently, a woman went one step further and asked to be photographed in a man's *wet* T-shirt.

When women feel they need a little help from a hairstylist or a makeup artist, Ryan arranges them on request. "I don't like to make women up to look like Barbie dolls, though," she says. "I'd rather just bring out their natural selves."

Who Will Pose?

Who are these women who are courageous enough to display their natural selves? "Mostly professional women," Ryan says. "A banker, a teacher, a newspaper reporter, an attorney . . ." A high percentage of her customers own their own businesses. Most of them are independent, self-confident women who want to give a gift of themselves to the man in their lives.

Sometimes it's the other way around. A man can purchase a gift certificate from Ryan so that she can capture how beautiful his woman is in his eyes. Maybe Ryan can help her to attain some self-confidence if she is unsure about her attractiveness.

Advertising and Promotion

Ryan stresses her gender when advertising her boudoir photography, for an important reason. Most of the pictures are gifts for the man in a woman's life, and the first thing he'll want to know is who took these pictures of his nearly naked love. Not many men would be pleased to learn that a man took the pictures. Ryan's gender, her clients tell her, is an important asset.

Very conscientious about promoting her work to ensure that her business continues to grow, Ryan displays her photos in places where people are thinking "boudoir," like lingerie stores and adult supply shops. She also exhibits her erotic photography in her storefront window which, she says, brings in about 25 percent of her business.

The idea of erotic photographs in a storefront window might cause alarm in some neighborhoods. Even your friends and family might get the wrong idea. Ryan says her father had some serious questions about the nature of the work she is doing, and that her mother would have preferred her to concentrate on photographing families and children, but on the whole, they have come to accept that her work is erotic, not pornographic. Her mother gave Ryan a big vote of confidence when she presented her with a $5,000 check as start-up money to open a studio.

Costs and Fees

"I read recently that a photographer needs $25,000 to $35,000 to open up a studio," Ryan says. "It's a good thing I didn't know that then." She wasn't able to buy everything she wanted right at the beginning, but was able to get by with used office furniture and leased lighting equipment. For three years she sent her photos out for developing, but now has her own photo lab in her studio. Her gross income recently was about $38,000, so she feels she can afford to buy all the equipment she needs.

Knowing what to charge for photography can be a bit perplexing for some photographic entrepreneurs. Ryan, posing as a potential customer, called most of the professional studios in Seattle and asked for their prices. Then she set hers squarely in the middle: $65 for a one-hour setting with thirty-six shots, and $50 for each 8½" x 11" portrait that a woman chooses from her proof sheet. She charges extra for shooting on location; the amount depends on the travel time involved.

Price notwithstanding, there are usually a hundred aspiring photographers in every town for every one who actually succeeds in building a solid business. Ryan had taken a few courses, she had a camera and some lenses, but really what set her apart from the pack was her choice of the boudoir niche and her vision of the beauty and subtlety possible in erotic portraits.

Laurel Holliday

CUSTOM CATERING

An anniversary, birthday, engagement, and other special occasions are often opportunities to take that "special someone" out to dinner. The couple envisions a romantic setting with candlelight, music, the finest cuisine, and everything else that would be included to make that time memorable. Unfortunately, reality is often a crowded restaurant, poor service, over-cooked food, and a table near the kitchen door—all at a price that just about cleans out their wallet!

There is hope for romance, however. Couples can have that wonderful evening just as they imagined if they live near Jacqueline Ruiz and Shirley Pyndinski. With Dinner For 2, part of their business, Occasions Unlimited, they will host a dinner in any home complete with romantic atmosphere, the finest linens and china, fresh flowers, complimentary wine or sparkling cider, and a pre-selected gourmet meal. They provide all this at an affordable price ($55 to $105).

If you can cook sumptuous meals, perhaps you can follow Ruiz and Pyndinski's example and fulfill that vision of a romantic evening for couples in your area. The start-up costs are very low, and the profits quite pleasing.

Ruiz and Pyndinski act as their client's cook and hostess as they serve everything from soup to nuts. They even bring a table, allowing the dinner to be served in any room. In keeping with the romantic theme of their dinners, they bring a small silver bell with a Cupid figure on it. Ruiz and Pyndinski stay in the kitchen until their customer rings the bell for the next course to begin; this insures maximum privacy for the diners. "We tell our customers they have to ring for us if they want to be served," says Ruiz. "Our idea is to give them uninterrupted privacy and maybe even an opportunity to kindle some romance."

A Dinner For 2 evening, on the average, takes about two-and-a-half hours to set up, serve, and clean up. "When our customers are finished dinner, we clean up in a matter of minutes and quietly leave," says Pyndinski. "We like to leave our customers' kitchens as though we had never been there. Recently, one couple celebrated an anniversary with one of our dinners," Ruiz recounts. "When they finished, Shirley and I were packed and out of their kitchen in ten minutes. They never heard us leave. The woman called the next day to say how much she and her husband enjoyed themselves. She said they hardly realized we were there. She promised to tell her friends how great everything was!"

Besides Dinner For 2, Ruiz and Pyndinski also offer a complete catering service for weddings, open houses, parties (Mexican fiestas, Chinese banquets, Super Bowl parties), office parties, and retirement dinners. Ruiz is also available as a photographer. "For around $235," she says,

"I will take ninety to 100 photos in natural lighting. Usually a bride and groom will hire me because they will already have someone videotaping their wedding and reception, but cannot afford to have a formal photo package."

Ruiz and Pyndinski take orders for Christmas cookies as well. During the holiday season, they post notices on community bulletin boards, and give out flyers to employees at local companies. The entire week before Christmas they bake, wrap, and even deliver the cookies to their customers. During one Christmas season, they baked 200 pounds of cookies—almost 7,000 of them! They charge $3.75 per pound for their cookies and offer ten different varieties. "Jackie and I were up until 3 A.M. almost every night just baking," says Pyndinski.

With the special dinners, photography, cookies, and catering, Ruiz describes their business as a total entertainment consultant service. "We can serve as few as two, to several hundred people," says Ruiz. "The largest we have served so far was a sit-down dinner for 220 people."

Operating the Business

To reach customers, the women have run both classified and display ads, but the results were disappointing. A better response came from direct mailings. "We use a local directory that lists neighborhoods by real estate value, and mail brochures to people we believe would be interested," says Pyndinski. "We also mail to couples who have been recently engaged." Because of their excellent service and food, they are now getting customers through word-of-mouth referrals.

Pyndinski and Ruiz offer gift certificates for their Din-

ner For 2. "One couple who received a gift certificate as a
wedding gift used it to celebrate their first anniversary,"
says Ruiz. "The couple called and told us it was one of the
nicest gifts they received!"

Ruiz and Pyndinski shop for the best food prices, but
always make sure they get top quality food. They shop at
their favorite stores and take advantage of sales on items
that they might need that week. For larger dinners and
other catering services, they keep their costs down by
purchasing from food distributors. Food distributors are
not always happy in dealing with small businesses like
Occasions Unlimited. "Some of those distributors won't
even let their trucks off the parking lots unless they are
filled with a minimum of $500 worth of food," says
Pyndinski. Despite these obstacles, however, Ruiz and
Pyndinski have been able to keep their prices low, yet still
competitive with other caterers.

In setting their prices, they will usually double their
food costs. Then they will call other caterers to see how
their prices compare. Keeping their overhead low by working from their homes and doing all the work themselves,
Ruiz and Pyndinski have been able to offer their customers
services few competitors can match. When a potential
customer calls Pyndinski, she will send them menus and
prices. They are willing to adapt their menus for any diet
or whatever the customer prefers.

Keys to Success

Pyndinski recommends to anyone who is interested in
this type of business that they get some training from a
food service program like those found at many local tech-

nical schools. Then she suggests that a person should work for a time in some area of the commercial food service industry.

Ruiz and Pyndinski agree that the key to success in business is knowing how to treat people. "Being competent in your business and complimentary in dealing with your customers are two of those important keys," says Ruiz. Ruiz and Pyndinski's philosophy of business is, "We go the extra mile to keep you!" Such a hardworking philosophy is the reason why Occasions Unlimited is becoming so successful.

Priscilla Y. Huff

HANDMADE PILLOWS

Chances are, "Seek and ye shall find" is an all-too-familiar phrase to Wendy and Bob Geer. In fact, the Biblical quotation, ". . .seek and ye shall find; knock, and it shall be opened unto you," is a description of the way the Geers developed the enterprise they call Kingsland. Wendy and Bob Geer design and manufacture pillows—contemporary styles and elegant one-of-a-kinds—that are created of lush antique materials and inspired by 19th-century designs. It is not unusual for a Kingsland pillow to command a retail price of $450. Since Kingsland has been in operation, it has won contracts with a chain of home furnishings stores and with exclusive shops.

The Geers are located far off the "big time" commercial path. They live in a tiny town in a remote corner of northern New Hampshire. So, it is especially remarkable that after only seven months in business, they had seven employees and were earning enough to devote all their time to the venture.

Wendy has always enjoyed sewing and the idea of combining old fabrics into an elaborate pillow appealed to her. It was also a product she could handle at home—"an ideal situation because our son was very young and we only had one car," says Wendy. Using antique materials she had on hand, Wendy designed and fashioned a sampling of pillows. The search for outlets began, but not very successfully. The Geers sought out friends who lived in towns where exclusive gift shops were located. They then travelled to Massachusetts where they walked around Boston looking for shops that would provide appropriate outlets for the pillows.

"Walking the streets and dragging huge garbage bags filled with pillows was frustrating and humiliating," recalls Wendy. But the "seek and find" expedition to Boston paid off. An interior designer and a gift shop owner agreed to sell the pillows. Then it was back to the sidewalks of Boston and northern Connecticut. Again, the pillows attracted outlets, including friends and shops in a Vermont resort town. The pillows appealed to sophisticated shops, and buyers for a chain of home furnishing stores "liked the fact that we could supply one-of-a-kind pillows and assure constant variety. They also liked our designs and combinations of fabrics and colors. What we offered seemed to complement the look they wanted in their stores—a mixture of the new and the old, nostalgia and elegance," says Wendy.

Kingsland's antique-style pillows are distinctive. The top of the Kingsland line (the pillow retails at about $450) features the finest antique materials on both the front and back—crushed velvet, linen, smooth velvet, and paisley. When the home furnishings chain asked them to create pillows with a contemporary motif, the Geers designed a sculptural shape suggestive of the past in muted colors. Kingsland's contemporary designs retail for approximately $100. The current best seller is a puff pillow for sofas. To assure that Kingsland's pillow designs are in the mainstream, the Geers are conscientious about keeping on top of changing tastes and styles.

The Geers find a wide variety of the luxurious antique materials "absolutely everywhere," says Wendy. "People give them to us, we advertise, scour flea markets and antiques shops, and we attend rummage sales. We love the hunt; it's the best part of the business."

The Geers share responsibility for the designs. Wendy continues to do much of the sewing, and Bob is the manager of Kingsland. Bob deals with clients, financial aspects of the business, supervision of the employees, and meeting production deadlines.

The completion of the pillows is done by seven part-time employees who work in their own homes. One employee may work on puff pillows, another is given ovals, another closes all of the pillows. In this sparsely populated region, Wendy doesn't try to find employees with special skills. Instead, she seeks out competent sewers who enjoy the craft. "They work in their own homes and most of them have families, so we try to juggle their time around. But we do expect them to be ready to make adjustments in their home life to meet a deadline."

With the exception of client-seeking outings, Kingsland is a home-based business. Like their employees,

Wendy and Bob work at home. Most of the operation is based in one central room. Other parts of the house are earmarked for specific jobs. Fabrics are dyed in the kitchen sink, pillows are stored in bedrooms, and Bob cuts and stuffs pillows in the shed.

The Geers financed their venture with $2,000. The money was needed, primarily, for the purchase of materials and to support production. Current costs, reports Wendy, average 40 percent of the amount received for each pillow, and can almost be equally divided between the costs of labor and materials. The completion of a pillow requires approximately two hours of labor.

Mildred Jailer

HOME MINI-FARM

Kona Kai Farms' half-acre location in Berkeley, California, grossed nearly $200,000 one year, a figure that owner Michael Norton claims makes it the most productive farm per acre in the United States. Using high-yield, "intensive" gardening methods such as the use of greenhouses, closer spacing, raised beds, and a rich, heavily composted soil, Kona Kai Farms raises some thirty varieties of edible flowers, thirty-plus varieties of lettuce, an assortment of salad greens and root crops such as Chioggia beets, Flambo radishes, and Paris Market Round Carrots. The produce is picked in the morning and delivered within hours to Bay Area restaurants like Masa's, Broadway Terrace, and Lalime's, and is shipped by Federal Express to the executive dining room of Shearson-Lehman Brothers in New York City.

Kona Kai is at the forefront of the new wave of small farmers making healthy profits from fresh, high-quality, specialty produce. Since the labor intensive, hands-on techniques required to turn out high-quality produce make it more adaptable to small farms rather than corporate farms, small-scale entrepreneurs have been quick to fill the market niche.

How to Start; What to Grow

According to Craig Wallin, author of *Backyard Cash Crops*, the advantages of growing on small acreage are many:

- You can start at home—even in your backyard.
- You can start with little capital.
- You can start in your spare time.
- Many crops are recession proof.

Growers with only a basement or garage can even consider growing sprouts or mushrooms. For example, Leslie Labowitz-Starus of Venice, California, grows sprouts (lentil, buckwheat, clover, radish, sunflower, wheat-grass, and a variety of bean sprouts) in her backyard, and sells to gourmet shops, farmers' markets, co-ops, and health food stores.

Wallin also advises small growers to concentrate on plants that the big wholesalers have overlooked because they require special care, but for which there is always a market. Herbs and organic fruits and vegetables, for example, are labor-intensive crops that do not lend themselves easily to large scale commercial farming operations.

According to Jeri Roderick, owner of Sunsprout Company, in Fairfield, Iowa, growing sprouts is a unique, high-margin business that a grower can start for under $2,500. "Every store, restaurant and food service is a potential customer," says Roderick. "A part-time grower, working ten to fifteen hours per week, can net weekly profits of $100 to $200."

Herbs are another potential big money-maker for small growers. According to Richard Miller, author of *The Potential of Herbs as a Cash Crop*, some large chain stores have called herbs "the fastest growing commodity in history." Maureen Buehrle, Executive Director of the International Herb Growers and Marketers' Association, claims that potpourris and flowers are two herbal markets that have a lot of profit and growth potential. Herbs are marketed also for medicinal purposes to pharmaceutical companies, or as spices and flavoring in cooking.

Another hot trend today is health foods, especially organic produce grown without pesticides or chemical fertilizers. According to Dr. Jeffrey Bland, president of HealthComm, Inc., a company specializing in health promotion and research, studies show that more and more people are considering health and diet as a factor in choosing their foods.

Marketing

Traditional farmers, accustomed to government subsidies and wholesale selling, have grown lazy about marketing, but the "new" farmer is a sharp marketer. Potential markets for various specialty products include garden centers, nurseries, florist shops, local grocery stores, gourmet shops, and health food stores. Other avenues include:

- Selling directly to restaurants, hospitals, schools, nursing homes, or hotels.
- Selling through specialty wholesalers or distributors.
- Selling at trade shows, county fairs, or craft fairs.
- Establishing pick-your-own produce patches or a roadside stand.

Farmer's markets are another major outlet, as consumers are always looking for locally grown, seasonal produce, and are willing to pay well for it. They enjoy meeting the farmers who grow the food they eat; the growers, in turn, receive direct feedback about the crops they're raising. Mail order can be risky for those not willing to do their homework in this highly competitive business, but the returns can be high for suitable products such as dried herbs and flowers, and value-added produce such as preserves and herbal sachets.

According to Mel Bartholomew, author of *Cash from Square Foot Gardening*, the best market for the backyard grower is restaurants. "They buy everything you can deliver, and pay you top retail prices—in cash on the spot," says Bartholomew. Major restaurant concerns are: freshness and quality; organic produce grown without pesticides; specialty produce not available in wholesale markets; and reliable, consistent delivery.

Specialty Crops: Minimizing the Risks

"Growers often are attracted to specialty crops because of the potential for hefty returns," says Conrad Leslie, publisher of the *Leslie Crop Report*. "But higher performance crops can carry matching risks." Frieda Caplan, one of the nation's leading specialty produce marketers, advises prospective specialty growers to: first go to a farm adviser in your area to find out what crops do best in your local climate and soil; check with wholesalers, distributors, and store owners to find out if there is a market for what you plan to grow; start out small and experiment.

Caplan also advises growers to diversify in crop varieties, not only as insurance against individual crop failures, but as a hedge against the trendy ups and downs of specialty markets. But the main requirement is to have a marketing plan. "So many growers go at it backwards," says Caplan. "They go plant, then go find the person to sell it for them. You just can't do that."

Roderick, owner of Sunsprout Company, advises prospective sprout growers as well as most specialty crop markets:

• Assess your potential customer base. Conduct a telephone survey to get a general picture of current market volume, price, sources, and quality.

• Contact restaurants and cafeterias which feature salad bars or gourmet sandwiches.

• Go to stores throughout your area. Talk to the produce manager and find out what he thinks of the sprouts carried, how much they sell for, and if there is interest in other varieties of sprouts or specialty products.

• Finally, stick with it.

Vance Merrill, California Direct Marketing Specialist, sums it all up: "Growers as well as the rest of the economy are recognizing the fact that there are a substantial number of customers who are demanding quality and service and are willing to pay for it."

For More Information

Check first with your local county extension office, then contact state and federal offices: Marketing Research and Development Division, USDA, AMS, Room 130, Bldg. 307-BARC-E, Beltsville, MD 20705.

Eric Gibson

HOMEMADE JEWELRY

Almost everyone has a box of sparkling old buttons from Grandma's sewing chest to marvel at, or a set of dominoes, checkers, or mah-jongg pieces rescued from a flea market. Maybe they have a partial Scrabble® game and perhaps even a collection of colorful, fifty-one-to-a-deck playing cards purchased at an antique store tucked away in a drawer. Gather your treasures together and start earning extra income now! Strap those buttons on a piece of elastic to create eye-catching bangle bracelets. Glue the dominoes, checkers, and Scrabble® pieces onto earring or pin backs for guys and gals. Whatever the material, mount your artwork on one-of-a-kind playing cards for good money in a rewarding home jewelry business.

In addition to having the satisfaction of creating fun gifts for family and friends out of "heirloom" materials, once the word is out, relatives will often send along their extra buttons and collectibles. This helps build an inventory, resulting in a minimal investment for supplies. The season for successful jewelry selling is year-round, since the pieces make wonderful birthday and Christmas gifts, as well as fun wardrobe accessories anytime. Men, women, and children can wear these button, domino, and checker pins and earrings, so the sky is the limit for profits. And this business can be worked out of your home part- or full-time.

Bev Rice is one designer who not only models what she sells, but delights in the pleasure others have in purchasing her sporty art. She and her husband Jim started a home business called "Sport in Life" ten years ago with one imperfect mah-jongg set originally bought as a present for a friend. In the past five years Sport in Life has evolved from marketing craft-fair products to bona fide antique buttons sold at a more expensive retail-quality level. With mostly word-of-mouth advertising, their jewelry has captured creative awards, been featured in the Image section of her local Sunday newspaper, displayed for sale in clothing and curio boutiques, and sold at jewelry parties.

Bev wanted to combine her love of going to flea markets with creative, artistic urges. While she comes up with her signature creations, Jim perfects ever-sturdier ways of fastening pieces together and drills holes in the mah-jongg tiles for Bev to thread with elastic to make bracelets or neck amulets. Earrings and pins can be made without drilling, however. Just purchase an inexpensive glue gun from the neighborhood hardware store, or sturdy "glue dot" stickers, as well as earring and pin backs, available wholesale. "Anyone can do this," says Bev.

Investment

Bev estimates start-up costs to be less than $500. Don't underestimate the value of trading services or receiving supplies when starting out. An artist friend created a simple but effective domino logo, and another friend who was teaching a printing class made up 500 business cards as a gift. Initially, Bev spent $100 per month on supplies. That included game pieces, pin and earring backs, and glue. The most interesting pieces can be found at thrift stores, flea markets, and garage sales.

Buying Supplies

Finding supplies can be time-consuming at first, says Bev, but all supplies can be bought in one's own neighborhood or ordered from supply catalogs. Her inventory is now built up, but when she first started out she went to stores three or four times a day to be the first person there and check on items arriving during the day. With vigilance and luck, "finds" can be snapped up as they get put on the shelves. Also, friends who peddle their wares at flea markets might bring her a mah-jongg set because they know exactly the kinds of things she uses.

To record money earned and money spent, and to keep track of what pieces are on consignment or out for a jewelry party, Bev recommends keeping an inventory sales book. She reports that generating $10,000 per year part-time is possible, while she estimates $30,000 to $40,000 could be made full-time, depending on effort and expertise. The qualities of integrity, flexibility, and enthusiasm are personal attributes that will make for better business, but being an artist is not a requirement.

What to Charge

Jewelry prices depend on time, materials, and what the

market will bear. Simple Scrabble® pins make great holiday stocking stuffers or children's birthday party favors and sell for $1.50. Antique button pins that look wonderful on a blazer lapel can start at $25 and well-made button bracelets can retail for between $25 and $50, depending on quality. Domino earrings and pins can run from $16 to $26. Vintage collectible mah-jongg and bamboo bracelets may wholesale from $88 to $250.

Methods of Selling

Jewelry parties. Although there is a variety of ways to sell jewelry, from craft fairs and festivals, at gift and clothing boutiques, on consignment or by personal referrals, the best methods really depend on individual preferences. There are benefits and pitfalls to each. For those starting out, Bev highly recommends holding jewelry parties as a fun, tried-and-true way to sell. Better yet, ask friends to hold them at their houses, serve a little something to eat and drink, and invite a group of about six to twelve people. In her experience, earnings of approximately $300 to $400 can be made from a home jewelry party.

Networking. Another method is to network with a friend to find trustworthy places that will take a chance on your work. This includes consignment at clothing or gift boutiques and possibly museum or art gallery gift stores, where a percentage of the profits are kept by the store upon sale. "Most rewarding," says Bev, "is when stores buy outright, because it keeps your cash flow going."

Crafts fairs. Crafts fair profits are tied into the costs of entry fees, booth space rental, and transportation to the fair. Some fairs require the artists to be present to sell their work. Depending on regulations, this can pose problems for the jewelry maker who has hired a sales representative. Sales generally depend on the ability of the individual seller and the quality of the neighboring crafts to help draw customers. Sometimes a percentage of sales goes for a worthy fundraiser. Also, many artists really enjoy displaying their wares in a festival atmosphere where they get a chance to meet and learn from each other.

Festivals. Unique designs, together with the touchable and playful qualities of the jewelry, are the strongest selling points at festivals and craft fairs. A small show may only charge a $50 entry fee and a net profit of $200 out of $400 gross sales is possible.

Fashion shows. Bev is occasionally invited to display her jewelry as part of vintage fashion shows where a friend is already selling and the artists dress up in appropriate period costumes. Or she might do a weekend show where she is given space to set up in a clothing boutique where a sale has been advertised. The store often sends out postcards notifying customers of the sale and perhaps a flyer noting an artist appearance. Bev says that she enjoys these, but points out that the store claims 30 percent of her sales. Also, selling all weekend can be very demanding.

Personal referrals. Since Bev has been in business for more than ten years and knows her market, she understands how her pieces sell best, and certainly what is cost-effective for her business. Personal referrals now account for 30 to 50 percent of Sport in Life sales, and 30 percent is repeat business. Someone starting out may need to try all avenues to see what kind of customers are attracted to a particular jewelry style. Besides word-of-mouth referrals by friends, and boosting sales by wearing the jewelry, a jewelry representative can bring up the bottom line of profit. Bev estimates that referrals from a rep who worked for her several years ago added another 10 percent to sales.

Paula Nichols

KIDS' SPORTS CARDS

For over thirty years, kids and adult sports fans have collected baseball cards. They are an enduring icon in American culture. Imagine, then, the thrill that a Little Leaguer would experience to see his own picture and stats on a custom-made baseball card. Every neighborhood has its share of Little League baseball teams and school teams, and customized baseball cards, designed for the players on these teams, are an item you can easily manufacture and sell—to the tune of $20,000 a year!

How to Start

You will need a good 35mm camera, preferably a single-lens reflex with close-up lens attachments. If you don't have one, you can purchase one for around $300. You'll also need a camera copy stand (about $100), and a small paper cutter which you can probably pick up for under $50. You will also have expenses for commercial artwork on your first cards. Aside from these expenses, however, all you will need is a sample baseball card which you will manufacture, and the necessary business licenses for your area. Your total start-up costs will be less than $1,000 in most instances, yet this is a sideline business which could easily generate as much as $20,000 to $25,000 per year in income.

Your first step is to approach as many prospects as possible with your sample baseball card. Make appointments to take the players' photos, preferably the whole team in one session. Try to keep them interesting. Avoid static poses, try for action shots as these will make the cards more appealing.

Making the Cards

The next step is to create the look of a baseball card from these photos. To do this, you will have to superimpose a team logo design over the front of the photo. You will need to have logos designed for each of your customers' teams. You can contact a local commercial artist to do this work, or you can hire the services of a talented art student. Logos should be designed in full color, and be original. Although most local teams do use the names of major league ball teams, such as Tigers, Reds, Cubs, and similar names, you will not want to infringe on the copyright of these major league baseball logo designs. Keep in mind that the money you spend in having these team logos designed is a one-time expense. Once you have the logos, you can use them over and over, season after season.

Take the logo and have photographic copies cut out and pasted to the front of a sheet of clear acetate. You can purchase acetate from most stationery or art supply stores. You can now place the acetate sheet over the top of the baseball picture you have taken. With the close-up lens attachment on your camera, re-photograph the original photo with the logo overlay. The resulting photograph will become the front side of your baseball card.

On the back side of the card you will want to put player statistics, which are furnished to you at the time of the photo session. These might include the child's name and age, the name of his team, the position he plays on the team, batting averages, and any other information you might wish to include.

To prepare the back side for printing, group several players to a page. Type all the statistics neatly into an area of about 2½" x 4½", leaving plenty of white space around the typed area. Space them equally on the page. You should be able to fit the statistics for about four players on each page. Now you take these typed pages to your local printer and have them printed on gummed paper. Have him print a small quantity—perhaps twenty-five or fifty— of each page, or whatever amount you will need to fill the customers' orders.

Next, cut out these statistics and paste them to the back of the player's photo, taking care to insure that the typed information is spaced even with the center of the photo and leaving plenty of white space at the edges. After you have pasted the two together, you will trim the cards in your paper cutter, making the final baseball card 3" x 5".

You should sell the cards in packages with about twenty cards in each. Cards can be priced at about 75¢ to a $1 each. Your cost to produce the cards will be approximately 25¢ to 40¢ per card. The rest is profit.

Every child on a team and every parent of a child on a team is a prospect. With a little salesmanship, you might be able to make the job easier by enlisting the aid and cooperation of your local Little League and school boards. In some instances, they may already be contracted to the services of another photographer for school and team pictures, but there is nothing to stop you from asking to bid on these assignments in the future in addition to furnishing them with your services in manufacturing the player cards. If you cannot work through the Little League and the schools, you still have the option of selling the baseball cards to the players and parents directly.

Other potential clients include junior high, high school, and college teams, and corporate softball leagues. Of course, you're not limited to baseball either. Consider providing the same product for football teams, basketball teams, soccer teams, and bowling leagues. With all these prospects, it could become a full-time business.

If you enjoy photography and sports, this is an excellent way to make those hobbies profitable.

Ron Coleman

LUNCH SERVICE

People working in the average office building face frustration every day because there just are not that many lunchtime options available to them. They can stand in a crowded cafeteria line, if there even is one, or buy whatever may be left in the food machines, or rush out to a restaurant and fight the noon-time crowds with one eye on the clock . . . or eat something they brought from home, which has probably grown soggy. The person who wants to enjoy the outdoors is often forced to give up having a good lunch at all in order to get an hour in the sun. The person who wants to use lunchtime for catching up on his work faces a different problem. He must either go hungry or spend most of the hour going out to buy food.

There's a way you can provide a much-needed service for all these people and make money, too. You can become a sandwich vendor, selling lunches desk-to-desk in an office building. Your customers will be able to use their lunch hour as they choose, free from the pressures and wasted time of locating their food. There are opportunities for this service in most areas having office buildings.

You will need to be free in the morning to make the sandwiches you'll sell, or work together with someone else who can do this part of the operation. The only investment necessary is in the sandwich ingredients. Here are two examples of how a successful lunch service can work:

1. John T. enrolled at his community college to learn the business of small appliance repair. When he finishes the program, he plans to open his own shop. Meanwhile, he pays his tuition and supports his family as a sandwich vendor. Each morning John and his wife make five dozen sandwiches and pack them into a large picnic basket. Leaving home at 11 A.M., John makes two stops: at an insurance company's

regional headquarters and at a medical/professional building. He finishes selling by 12:30 P.M. and has plenty of time to reach his afternoon classes at college. Each week he clears about $300.

2. Carmen G. lives in an apartment with her two children. After seeing them off to school each day, she makes forty sandwiches in her small kitchen. Carmen has developed a system for using her limited counter space efficiently and finishes in less than two hours. With the sandwiches neatly packed into a carrier, she walks a few blocks to a street of small retail businesses, where the owner/operators are unable to leave their shops for lunch. Carmen's daily profit is $35, or about $700 a month. She gets home well ahead of her children's return from school. Three times a week the family goes shopping together for ingredients.

When a service is operated as a partnership, one person—for example, a retiree or a shut-in—makes the sandwiches, and a second person sells them. The vendor can even be working regular daytime hours and devoting his own lunchtime to the project.

Getting Started

The first step is to analyze your market. Select two or three office buildings and look closely at what the people working there do for lunch. Spend time visiting these areas around noon. If possible, talk with some of the employees.

Describe the service you plan to start and listen to their comments.

If none of the buildings seems right, you might consider working two smaller buildings that are close to each other, a small business district, or a downtown college without food service. A surprising number of specialized schools, such as those that teach art, design, music, dance, ballet, and office skills, do not have space to provide eating facilities. Finally, choose the buildings most in need of your service.

Find out whether any special entrance pass is required. Talk with the office manager, or whoever is responsible for building security and explain your business plans. Most people will welcome your service, but because it is new, you may occasionally meet resistance at the beginning. Listen to any objections with an open mind, and answer each point directly. For example, a supervisor may think the presence of a salesperson in the office will be distracting. You can point out that your service will help reduce the number of people returning late from lunch and may encourage some to work during part of their noon break, especially on poor-weather days. Since every manager wants a more efficient operation, this argument can be a strong selling point. If you discover that the building you have selected has unusually strict regulations, such as no eating at desks, it is probably better to change your choice of location.

Find out exactly when the lunch hour begins in all the offices. A large building may house several different companies, each with its own schedule. Take notes for future reference.

Announcing Your Service

Let your potential customers know your service will be starting soon. One good way to announce your plans is with a poster on the office bulletin board or in the elevator. Be sure to see if you need a clearance stamp on it before putting it up. You might want to include a sample menu and prices. Put the date your service will begin on the poster. It is usually best to make your announcement about one week ahead so that the information has time to sink in. If possible, follow up the poster with a reminder on the day before your service begins. You may even want to photocopy individual flyers for each desk if this agrees with established office policy. Be sure to describe your menu in taste-tempting language. From a psychological standpoint, the ideal time to distribute this announcement is immediately before lunch, when people are hungry and food sounds most appealing.

In most situations, the best day of the week to start your service will be Tuesday. If you begin on a Monday, your reminder will have been made the Friday before—too long a time for people to remember it clearly. Tuesday also gives you four consecutive days to begin developing regular customers.

Selecting the Menu

The service should offer at least four, and probably no more than eight, types of sandwiches. Each should be prepared on at least two choices of bread—one light and one dark. These quantities will give people a good selection without overwhelming them. Your sandwich fillings should be more imaginative than what someone might slap together at home for himself. Avoid the boring kinds, like peanut butter, cold cuts, and plain cheese. Tempting sandwiches should not be unusual. Test the recipe for each filling yourself, and ask for opinions from family and friends. Blends such as tuna salad or egg salad must not be runny or sloppy; people eating them may be dressed up or working around important papers. Plan to include at least one non-meat sandwich to balance your menu. Don't skimp on ingredients. If you make your sandwiches from the finest products and give each customer a bit more for his money than he's used to, repeat sales are more likely.

Planning Ahead

Sit down with paper and pencil. When you have worked out your menu and the recipes, plan how many of each kind of sandwich to make each day. After a week or so, you will be able to base this decision on sales patterns. At first, use your best judgment. Next, list all the ingredients you'll be using. Estimate how much of each you will need per week. Take time to visit supermarkets and compare prices of the ingredients. Plan to buy meats and cheese sliced by a delicatessen unless you own a professional slicing wheel. See if there is a bakery outlet store in your area. If so, test the freshness of its merchandise. Prices at these outlets are usually half of retail. Consider purchasing large, institutional sizes of ingredients you will use frequently, such as mayonnaise. With this information, make a shopping list for the week, and schedule your buying trips.

Look at your notes about when lunch starts in the

offices you are servicing. Plan to arrive about fifteen to thirty minutes before this time. This is when people are still at their desks, and everyone is getting hungry. Also, it will take you at least fifteen minutes to circulate through a small building. Work backwards from this arrival time to develop a schedule for your morning.

Setting Menu Prices

Using your planning lists, work out your actual cost for each sandwich. The price at which you sell it should be about two or two-and-a-half times the cost of your ingredients. Estimate a retail price for each sandwich and compare this to the average charge at area restaurants. You may find you can increase your price slightly and still be competitive. On the other hand, you may want to reduce some of the prices a little for the same reason. If there is any sandwich variety that will be unprofitable for you to sell, drop it from your menu.

The night before the first day of service, double-check to see that you have purchased all necessary ingredients in sufficient quantities. Allow yourself plenty of time in the morning since some of the steps in sandwich making may take longer than you expect. Keep ingredients wrapped and refrigerated until you need them. This will make everything taste fresher. It is also better to finish one sandwich at a time rather than to spread out many slices of bread and have them dry out before you can fill them.

Each sandwich should be wrapped in a plastic bag, or in cling wrap. Always use clear material so the customer can see the merchandise. Prepare labels in advance, and attach one to the sandwich at the same time it is wrapped.

Labels should be neatly printed, typed, or photocopied. Refrigerate all finished sandwiches until you are ready to pack them. This will be your final step before leaving the house. The carrying case you use should have a wide opening so customers can look at their choices easily. It should be designed to travel upright. It needn't be new but should be in good condition.

Your appearance is also very important. Customers will judge your product in part by how you look. Be sure to take plenty of change with you, both coins and single dollar bills. There probably will not be any place for you to have money changed at the office.

When you arrive, it is a courtesy to tell the supervisor that you're there. Be proud of your sandwiches and your service. Let each potential customer look at your wares. Answer his or her questions, and describe your merchandise with enthusiasm, but don't try to pressure people into buying. If the sandwiches are appealing, they will sell. Notice what varieties are most popular. As days and weeks pass, you will find yourself with regular customers. Try to begin your sales route with them so you won't run out of their favorite before you get to them. If this isn't possible, keep a few sandwiches in reserve to fill their orders.

Additions to Your Service

You may want to add a paper plate and napkin as a free part of the service. It is possible to wrap a sandwich directly on a paper plate, but this will take up more room in your carrying case and may cause part of the filling to slip out in transit. At the beginning, it is usually best to limit your menu to sandwiches. After you have tested the market, however, you may want to add new lines. These might include individual bags of potato chips, dessert items, or beverages. They will be primarily for customer convenience because your profits on such lines will be much smaller. They will also take up space and add weight to your carrying hamper.

If you introduce a new sandwich variety or a dessert, it is good public relations to prepare small free samples for each customer. This will acquaint them with the new product and help build sales. In regions of the country where health foods are popular, or if several potential customers are on weight-control diets, you may want to add a salad to your menu. Sturdy paper bowls (sold with picnic supplies) are the best containers. To take advantage of seasonal produce, call the salad something like a "garden delight" or "low-calorie special" and vary the composition of the dish from month to month. You can also create a health sandwich from garden produce.

MAIL ORDER

If you have a big, fat bankroll you can start out in mail order with a lavish advertising campaign in all the media. You can produce a four-color catalog on slick paper, and purchase expensive mailing lists and the newest automated equipment. You can hire skilled and experienced employees, and you can import or manufacture attractive, expensive products. All you would require is a great deal of cash.

However, if a great deal of money doesn't happen to be one of your current surplus possessions, you can still be successful in mail order. Thousands of people all across the country have started mail order businesses on shoestring budgets and are thriving today. This is the way we recommend that you start in your own mail order business: begin with a modest business and build it, step by step, into a full-time money maker. It takes practically no investment, but does require good judgment, a bit of luck and, most importantly, a plan.

While there are a number of routes that have worked well for small-investment beginners, the ten steps outlined here represent ones that have brought the most success to the most newcomers for the smallest outlay of cash. If you have big dreams about building a mail order business—but a nickel-and-dime budget as a foundation—this is the surest way to get off the ground.

Start With One Strong Product

The big mail order pros think a twenty-page catalog is small. In order to compete with retail outlets and the other mail order houses, they say, you've got to have a full line. And if your products are similar or identical to the ones that crowd the counters in department stores and gift shops, that's true. On a small budget, however, a big, diversified line isn't feasible. The solution is to start with a single product or with a group of closely associated products. In either case, they should be unique, individual, or unavailable elsewhere. That might sound like a tough order, but it's not as limited as it might seem. Anything homemade, handmade, custom-made, imaginative, or special would fall into this category.

Today there are many successful single-product mail

order businesses, and in each case the keystone of their success is the product. Some examples: custom-designed weather vanes; hand-hooked rugs; packets of seed from Indiana's famous Golden Raintree; hand-engraved stationery; and sports car motif jewelry.

Note that in each case the nature of the product takes away the likelihood of serious competition from other sales outlets. In some cases, for example, the products are regional; that is, they are unavailable in most parts of the country. Others are rather special in their appeal; in a medium-sized town there wouldn't be enough demand for them to support a retail outlet. Others are unique because of the individual craftsmanship it takes to produce them.

Note also that most of them can be produced on order, so that there's no need to invest in big, expensive inventory. And, to support the cost of mail order promotion, the products should be saleable at a price that's at least three times your wholesale cost, or the cost of materials and labor (even if the labor is your own).

Test Before You Invest

In any given year, the U.S. government is likely to issue half a dozen patents for cigarette packages, cases, or holders that incorporate some kind of receptacle for ashes and cigarette butts—each patent representing a different way of skinning that particular cat. Trouble is, practically none of them reach the market. The public apparently doesn't care if the cat never gets skinned at all. The moral is plain: a workable idea isn't necessarily a saleable idea. Before you invest a substantial amount of money in promoting *any* product, give it a market test. Even on a small scale, ads in national publications cost too much for the budget-bound beginner to use them as a testing ground. A much better idea is to use inexpensive *local* advertising, or test run an ad in a local retail outlet, or both.

For a test in a retail store, find a shop (usually either a gift shop or a specialty shop) that's reasonably appropriate for your product. Tell the owner what you're doing, offer him an extra discount, or if necessary, ask him to take your samples on consignment. For a fair test of its general sales appeal, be sure your product goes out on the shelves like any other item, with no special handling or display.

For an inexpensive test of its ability to sell through advertising alone, find a nearby newspaper that has both moderate rates and a weekly or daily "shoppers' page" or "shoppers' column" devoted mostly to mail order items. Shopper papers like *PennySaver* are good ad vehicles. If possible, run an ad with approximately the same copy, photo, and dimensions you plan to use later in your national advertising.

Find the Right Media

Some beginners sell their products by direct mail using flyers, brochures, and samples, plus lists of names bought from list brokers. Most, though, find it's more practical and profitable to build their own lists of buyers by advertising in national publications. The crucial point is finding the right publications. Ad rates are based largely on circulation: the more readers a publication has, the higher its rates are. But *numbers* of readers don't necessarily tell the whole story in mail order. Consider, for example, an ad for the sports car motif jewelry noted above. In a big general interest publication, many readers would see it, but only a small percentage would be interested enough in sports cars to care. In a man's magazine, the number of readers might be smaller, but the percentage of response would probably be higher. In a sports car magazine, the readership would be still smaller, but the percentage of response should be highest of all. Since its ad rates would also be the lowest of the three, it should clearly be the best spot for the kickoff advertising.

All this may seem obvious, but thousands of mail order beginners have overlooked it. Not the successful ones, though. In fact, many experienced mail order people won't even consider a given product unless they know they have "somewhere to go with it"—a special interest magazine or other ad medium where they can get *selected* readership that matches the product—and at a relatively low cost.

Media evaluation takes plenty of comparative research, and you can do a lot of it by poring over *Standard Rate and Data,* a directory (available in the reference section of most public libraries) that lists all the publications in the country and indicates both circulation and ad rates. Besides that, any publication will gladly send you rate cards on request, and many will help you compose an ad with "pull."

Get Free Promotion

In order to produce a selling ad, you need strong, concise copy (the written description) and generally a good—that means professionally shot—photo. With the same ingredients, you can often get thousands of dollars' worth of free promotion for your product by preparing a news release. Since advertising is likely to be the biggest single item in the mail order budget, the gratis type is well worth going after.

Many national publications give free space to interesting new products, but for every release they use, a dozen are rejected. To make sure your press release gets top consideration, make your copy informative and as interesting as possible, concentrating on any newsworthy details. Keep the copy short and concise, two paragraphs is about the right length. The copy should be double-spaced with wide margins, and carefully typed. If you send it out in volume, have it professionally photocopied or printed. Be sure it includes a mailing address and product price.

Hire a good photographer to shoot pictures of the product, but order prints from a company that specializes in quantity processing. Most large cities have such photo services; use the *Yellow Pages* and check around for prices. The prints should be glossy and a minimum of 4 x 5 inches. To keep costs down, order four 4 x 5's printed on a single 8 x 10 sheet, and cut them later; in that form, you ought to be able to effect a substantial savings.

The press release should go out to as many publications as you can afford to hit. You'll start, naturally, with the ones whose readers are likeliest to regard your product as newsworthy, but if your budget allows some leeway, don't stop there; news releases often score in some very unlikely publications.

Be Ready for Business

The big moment in mail order comes when the orders start rolling in, but too many beginners take a beating because they're not ready for it. It's important to fill orders promptly, and that means making advance arrangements for extra product materials, packaging materials, and maybe for extra help. Don't lay in excess supplies: do have lines of supply open, so that you can avoid having to arrange for materials and help under pressure, and paying premium prices for sudden service. These are important points in terms of economy.

If in spite of advance planning you get more orders than you can fill immediately, or if there's any other reason for delay in filling the order, be sure to acknowledge the orders—particularly the ones specifying C.O.D.—with a photocopied or pre-printed postcard that tells the customer he'll be getting his merchandise soon.

Keep Careful Records

The orders you get are an end in themselves, but they're more than that. For one thing, they represent the best market research you'll ever get. To make the most of it, each ad you run should be carefully "keyed"—that is, the address printed in the ad should include code letters or numbers (like "Dept. DS-1"). Use a different code for each publication and each issue, and for every variation of copy, price, etc., that you use in your advertising. By keeping careful records as the orders come in, you'll soon find out which qualifications, issues, and copy phrases pull best for you. By keeping track of all the details, you can learn which ads produce more C.O.D.'s, returns, etc.

Note this, too: When all the returns are in on a given ad, divide the cost of the ad by the total number of paid orders it produced. That gives you the most important single statistic in your business: the cost of advertisement per sale. When you know that, you know where to go next.

Build Your List

The orders and inquiries you get have still another function. The names and addresses on them become part of a priceless business asset: your own "selected" list of high-potential future customers—people who responded once to your wares, and probably will again. As you start adding to your line, the names on that list will be your hottest prospects for follow-up.

Add Products to Your Line

Always be on the lookout for new products to add to your line, but keep them in context. With one strong product established as the foundation, you're ready for the next step in the block-by-block building of a mail order business: the cautious addition of more products. Choose products that appeal to approximately the same buyers as your first one. The reason for choosing products with a common market are clear and compelling:

• You can advertise in the same media you tested out for the first product, thus avoiding most of the trial-and-error period.

• You can push two or more products in a single ad for the same cost.

• You can take full direct mail advantage of your list of previous customers.

Consider a Catalog

Some of the biggest mail order houses regard magazine advertising as simply a means of getting lists of good prospects for direct mail sales via catalogs. Others, equally big, rely almost entirely on magazine promotion (and maybe volume sales to jobbers), and never even get around to producing a catalog. To a large extent, the decision you make will depend on the type of products you're selling, and on the results of your cautious tests.

Don't Be Afraid to Grow

When you've come this far you're in the same class as the big-money beginner—only better, because you know you're on solid ground. At this point, don't be afraid to compete, and don't be afraid to grow. You may be able to expand by streamlining your operation with staff or automated equipment. Or maybe you'll want to invest in inventory: discontinued wholesale stocks, imports, etc. Keep your cost-accounting detailed and accurate, and move cautiously—but move.

For Further Information

How to Start Your Own Mail Order Business by the Editors of *Income Opportunities*. Davis Publications, 380 Lexington Avenue, New York, NY 10017. A complete 200-page, step-by-step manual covering every aspect of mail order, from choosing a name to creating your own catalog and everything in-between. Includes FREE publication, *How to Write a Classified Ad That Pulls;* $49.95 plus

$3.00 shipping and handling. Credit card orders call toll-free: 1-800-338-7531.

SIGN PAINTING

The best, most economical way to start out as an independent sign painter is to print up a nice flyer, a business card, and to purchase a small array of brushes. But before purchasing any paint inventory, wait to buy the right colors for that first job. These days computers can be used to produce letter stencils for commercial banners, but a lot of pride is still in the artistry of being able to create sandblasted or carved wooden signs that are popular in suburban and rural areas. Other signs use silk screening, spraying, or etching techniques.

"It is a great feeling to help materialize people's visions of their business with signs," says Hobart Swan, a custom sign painter. He has been in this low-overhead business for more than ten years and describes some of the ins and outs of working as an independent contractor. An artistic background is helpful, but what is really important is to have a sense of design and the mechanical ability to use the special brushes. Swan started out as an art student in Seattle with a graphics background, then joined an urban sign-painting union where he honed his color combination, composition, and layout skills.

Swan suggests that sign painting is an open field because there aren't many sign experts. He says that there is a lot of freedom in the work and he likens it to plumbers or electricians. "Every business needs signs, but they need help in articulating their visions of signs for their stores."

This is a good time to get into sign painting, asserts Swan, because the computer as a tool frees up a painter's time to use his or her talents for more interesting jobs.

Setting Up the Business

Little capital investment is required to start up. Swan suggests buying a table saw and drill that can be set up in a garage or basement. A small contractor has the time to go out and drum up business. In an urban area, one method is to put flyers out while canvassing the downtown area and to drop off business cards to businesses that have no signs or where a sign is in need of improvement. Or a new store may need a grand opening banner. Swan advises not taking on any job that is under $100 because it is just not cost effective.

The Design Process

While computers have radically changed the industry, Swan worries that some of the traditional skills of a craftsman in the design process will be lost in favor of technical mass production. Swan says that illustrations and cartoons, whether drawn freehand or with the help of a microcomputer software program, are more important than ever. But the customer from FiFi's Poodle Parlor still needs to see a thumbnail sketch of what her sign might look like. In Swan's experience, the one-on-one with people and executing personal designs is the fun part because individual creativity can come into play.

Working up a thumbnail sketch is the first step in the design process. Maybe FiFi's needs a round wooden sign.

Thumbnail sketches can be worked up in about a week. But never charge for sketches if the customer does not want to place an order, says Swan, and be sure to get the sketches back. He says that it is easy to tell if someone is going to "rip you off" and have the original sketches reproduced or made camera ready. But if an order is taken, then be sure to add in a charge for the designs.

Swan suggests showing the potential buyer one basic sketch and one more elaborate design. For example, a $200 and a $400 sample. He also recommends "selling customers up," which means suggesting gold leaf detailing, silk screening or etching, and a fancier sign material. Or "high-end" sand-blasted, wood-carved signs can be promoted over "low-end" computerized lettering. "This is not greed," says Swan. "You want to make the customer satisfied."

Range of Materials

Aside from promotional banners, which can be constructed from paper or vinyl, signs on storefronts are made to be hanging a long time. The range of materials most often used are plywood, redwood, plexiglass, aluminum, or concrete. If plywood is the selected material, it must be "MDO," medium density overlay plywood. This is available at lumber supply or wholesale dealers for about $150 up to $500. Using untreated plywood with its rough surface is "the first sign of an amateur," according to Swan. Also, don't try to paint on canvas or cotton.

Again, don't stock up on any of these more costly items until the first order is placed. Eventually an array of brushes will be needed for the different painting surfaces.

But until the business gets going, only buy brushes on an individual basis. Swan points out that an "electropounce" stencil tool for lettering is something that may be required from the start. It costs about $200 and works "like a needle with a grip on it" to transform electromagnetic impulses into dents in metal.

The painting surface will determine what kind of paint to buy. Specific paints for lettering such as "Sho-card color" is what Swan uses most often. It is water-based and goes on fourteen-ply colored crescent board for menus, "For Sale" signs, and notices of special events. Poster color paint dries in one hour and has a matte finish, good for when a lot of different colors are needed, for one-day sales signs, or when Swan says, "someone calls at 2 P.M. and wants something by 4 P.M." Glossy enamel takes a day to dry and is often used for outdoor wood signs and banners and can cost between $10 and $20 per quart.

Learning Basic Techniques

In learning the mechanics of constructing signs and letters it is helpful to have some artistic skill or sense of design. Otherwise one's range of work will be limited to very basic projects. Of course, starting with the basics is what it is all about. Trade magazines and training or apprenticeship can provide invaluable assistance. Swan describes the benefits of reading *SignCraft* magazine for guidance in how to price signs, learn specialty techniques, and even for ordering materials. He says it is possible to invest in back issues to learn all aspects of the business.

The easy part may be in reading about techniques. The hard part is setting out to master them. Swan says learning how to use "quills, flats, soft fitches, and stiff bristles" is what separates the master sign painters from the apprentices. Stiff bristles are specialty brushes which are used on concrete, rough, unfinished wood and vinyl. Soft fitches are used on smoother surfaces. Brushes run anywhere from $15 to $20 each.

The quill is the hardest brush to learn to use, according to Swan. The best quills are actually Russian squirrel hairs bound to a goose quill, he explains. "Among sign painters, if you've learned how to use the quill," says Swan, "then you are probably a sign painter." But don't despair, assistance can be obtained in the form of video tape demonstrations ordered from *SignCraft* magazine.

Swan says the techniques that a high-end painter might use, such as the quill, are sometimes carefully guarded because they provide an edge up on the competition. But if one has the opportunity to become an apprentice or work for a sign shop, then exposure to silk screening, sand-blasting, or etching techniques is very likely. One frustration in working for a commercial shop, according to Swan, is that with more experienced people around it is sometimes harder to get the chance to work on the more difficult signs.

One standard way to get an apprenticeship training used to be to enroll in a union apprenticeship program as Swan did. He recalls that apprentices were taught to use "incredible" mother-of-pearl inlays along with traditional silver and gold leaf. Swan says these union opportunities are less available today, but with the advent of the computer even "non-creative" people can do signs.

At the same time, for those with creative aspirations and abilities Swan says there is a resurgence of requests for the high-end specialty designs. Even though "the computer can generate the most interesting patterns," as Swan describes it, "the sign painter has to be good enough to do it in the amount of time it takes to make it profitable."

Advertising; Permits

Walking around commercial areas and posting flyers at places in need of signs and handing out business cards are two methods of advertising. Swan recalls that in his first year he produced a really nice flyer at Christmas and went around offering to decorate storefront windows with watercolor paints for $200.

Display advertising is a good idea, says Swan, but it pays to check prices. Local newspaper display ads can run anywhere from $250 to $800 for a one-quarter-page ad, or $500 to $1,600 for a half-page ad. *Yellow Pages* advertisements start at a minimum of about $1,000. Although most papers will offer a size and frequency discount, perhaps the best way to build a business is through word-of-mouth advertising. After the first year it will be apparent which advertising methods generate the best results. By the same token, confidence and sign-painting skills will increase in the first few years. Swan estimates that in a rural area first-year earnings might be $12,000. In an urban area the figure might be closer to $20,000. "If you are serious about the business, a competent sign painter can clear $40,000."

Sign-painting permits vary from city to city, from no constraints to those requiring approval for exterior signs. Swan relates that it doesn't cost much to get a sign approved but fines can be imposed for those hung without a permit. Even worse, if local ordinances exist and a sign does not meet them, the owner can be asked to take down the sign. Swan says he is generally in favor of permits for the sake of more pleasing sign aesthetics.

The visual aesthetics are important, not just from a creative or mechanical standpoint, but in terms of good business. "To be a good sign painter," says Swan, " you have to be interested in the visual environment. If you have enough integrity to contribute to and improve the visual environment, you'll make a good business."

Paula Nichols

SPECIALTY ADVERTISING

You may not be familiar with the term "specialty advertising," but you are probably familiar with the products. Both at home and at work, we are surrounded by advertising specialties—functional items such as calendars, pens, key chains, and rulers imprinted with a business logo and advertising messages. These products represent a very profitable opportunity for creative salespeople. They are profitable because there is no investment in equipment (unless you choose to do the imprinting yourself; see below), so the cost of getting started in the specialty field is minimal, and overhead and expenses are low. Being a creative salesperson is an advantage because you'll need excellent sales ability and a good imagination to earn high profits.

If you don't already have strong selling skills, or a sincere desire to learn them, specialty advertising is not for you. But if you enjoy working with people, and are enthusiastic about the products you sell, then the ad specialty field can offer numerous rewards—including a potentially high income. Of course, the actual income you make from selling specialties will depend on many factors, including what items you sell, how large or small each order is, how much time and energy you invest in sales, and your business expenses. For example, there are reportedly 15,000 different products in the specialty field, ranging from pens to clocks, watches, and other "gift" items which retail for hundreds of dollars. This is not to say that inexpensive pens are not profitable, however. Inexpensive items are usually ordered in very large quantities, which can make the profits from these orders equal to profits from the sale of one or two gift items.

Advertising specialty distributors can earn over $100,000 a year, although this would be unlikely your first few years in business. With hard work and common business sense, however, it is reasonable to expect yearly sales to range from $10,000 to $50,000.

Before detailing how to start a profitable specialty advertising distributorship, let's take a closer look at how advertising specialties work.

What It Is, What It Does

Unlike newspaper, television, or radio advertising, it is not the media but the method which defines specialty advertising. An "ad specialty" could be any item that is imprinted with a slogan, logo, or ad message. What makes it an ad specialty is the fact that it is given away to the recipient without cost or obligation. Some of the most common products used as ad specialties are calendars, pens and pencils, glasses and mugs, office accessories, T-shirts, and jewelry. But this list is just the tip of the iceberg. Many other items, from toys to watches, can be employed as advertising specialties. The more creative and unusual the product, the more effective it is likely to be.

The customers who buy and use these products are nearly as diverse as the products themselves. Businesses, nonprofit organizations, and politicians are prime customers for specialties. They use ad specialties to: promote their image; introduce new products, locations, or services; increase sales; create good will; thank customers, salespeople, and employees; and generate trade show traffic.

Imprinted products are just a small part of specialty advertising. You could probably earn a decent living just selling specialty advertising products, and leaving it up to the customer on how they are used, but the most successful advertising specialty distributors go beyond product selling. They sell ideas and programs to increase the effectiveness of the product.

In brief, the ad specialty program involves five steps:

1. Start with a goal, such as to increase the number of visitors to a manufacturer's booth at a trade show.

2. Determine a target audience, such as dealers who have pre-registered for the show.

3. Select a theme, slogan, message, and distribution (for example, "ACME support = more sales + higher profit") imprinted on specialties which are mailed to dealers before the show, along with an invitation to visit the ACME booth.

4. Select products which best fit the program. For example, to relate to the above "support" theme, consider suspenders imprinted with a message and "$" signs. Dealers who bring their invitations to a trade show booth might receive a paperweight in the shape of hands holding up a "$" sign.

5. Instruct and aid the customers with distribution and follow-up. Measure results by counting the number of dealers who bring an invitation to the booth.

In order to see how these five steps are put into practice, let's take a look at a few specialty advertising programs. These programs received awards from the Specialty Advertising Association International's (SAAI) Pyramid competition.

Nonprofit Organization

Not-for-profit organizations often use specialty campaigns to raise funds or increase volunteerism. The American Red Cross's Northeast Region Blood Services implemented a specialty campaign to recruit more blood donors. The theme of the campaign, "Blood Buddies," supported the idea of encouraging a friend to donate.

The program was targeted toward students and faculty of high schools and colleges. On-campus organizers (volunteers) were given a mug imprinted with the theme "Famous Buddies Make a Difference" and a list of well-known "buddies" such as Romeo and Juliet. First-time donors were rewarded with a key ring imprinted with the Blood

Buddies theme, and each donor received a button with the message: "Become a Buddy for Life—Give Blood."

Political Campaigns

Politicians are perhaps the best known specialty users. As voting day nears, the number of buttons, banners, and balloons increase. In order to stand out in the mass of specialty promotions, it is important that political specialties be unique and creative. This doesn't mean that traditional specialties won't work. Often a twist on the traditional is the most eye-catching.

Business—Increase Sales

Specialty advertising is an ideal complement to other advertising media like newspapers and television. A Chicago supermarket instituted a specialty campaign to help reinforce their identity in these traditional media and generate more sales. The theme of the campaign consisted of a "mascot"—a cartoon-like grocery cart with the message "C'mon In and Push Me Around." Many different items were used including pens, yo-yos, and T-shirts. The promotion increased sales by 16.7 percent.

Business—Promoting Image

A restaurant which had been unsuccessful under several different owners was once again under new ownership. The new owners planned to hold a grand opening and decided to promote the "new image" of the restaurant with a specialty campaign. Taking a cue from the restaurant name, "For-key's," different fork-shaped or fork-imprinted items were used. A mailing to a select group of individuals included fork-shaped pens, imprinted matchbooks, and baseball caps. These items were also given away during the grand opening. According to the restaurant owner, the mailing had a 73 percent response rate and gross sales for that year were double the best previous year.

Business—Motivating Employees

Specialty advertising campaigns aren't just useful for promotions aimed at customers, however. Many companies have internal promotions aimed at employees and salespeople. One store that wanted to improve employees' attitudes toward customer service started a program which involved "friendly shoppers" who evaluated employee performance. Although the employees were informed about the "friendly shoppers," they had no way of knowing who they were.

If the employee was friendly, helpful, and said "thank you," the "shopper" awarded him or her with a lapel pin and key chain. When employees failed, they received a card encouraging them to do better in the future. According to the company, awards outnumbered failures three-to-one by the end of the campaign. The program also resulted in a reduction in the number of customer complaints.

These are just a few of the numerous ways specialties are being used creatively and effectively. These examples illustrate the value of not just selling customers an imprinted product, but in helping them design a campaign that will be truly effective.

How to Get Started

Since most suppliers will drop ship orders directly to your customers under your label, you don't need large storage facilities or inventory. Although most successful distributors do have a business location, you can easily start your distributorship from home. It may be possible to start the business as a part-time venture, but since your most profitable customers will be businesses you need to contact during regular hours, it would be difficult to successfully run a specialty advertising business if you hold a nine-to-five job.

The cost of starting up is minimal. You will need supplier catalogs, sample products, and ideas. You can find specialty suppliers in the *Thomas Register* (check your library), by attending one of the Specialty Advertising Association International's trade shows, or by considering the companies mentioned below. The trade shows can be attended by non-members for a higher registration fee.

Although you can be successful in the specialty field without joining SAA International (the specialty industry's nonprofit trade organization), it does have a strong influence over the industry and it is important to know about. Along with holding trade shows, the organization is also strong in promoting continuing education for its members and promoting professionalism in the industry. For more information about their services and membership contact: SAA International, 1404 Walnut Hill Lane, Irving, TX 75038-3094.

While most suppliers will send catalogs free of charge, you will probably want to purchase additional catalogs to distribute to customers. Some suppliers sell "blank" catalogs (without their name and address) with a space for imprinting your own business name and phone number. When collecting these catalogs, you will want to pay attention to information about the supplier. Most catalogs include a sheet which specifies shipping and billing procedures. Note if the supplier will drop ship orders to the customer. Some suppliers will ask for payment with an order, or will ship C.O.D. to new distributors. Write to companies you intend to do business with and supply them with your credit history in advance so that you can be billed for your initial order.

Also start learning about different suppliers' requirements for artwork and copy. Although the supplier will be doing the imprinting of products, you will need to send them the information. This may be a rough sketch or camera-ready artwork. Some suppliers require typeset copy, while others will set the type and need just the wording. Be aware of artwork charges or set-up charges on imprinting. You will need to include these costs in the price you quote the customer.

Getting Customers

You will want to have a fairly wide selection of sample products from various suppliers so that the customer can see the actual item. A few suppliers will send sample kits free, some will send samples at a nominal charge, and some reimburse this charge on your first order. You can build up your selection of samples as your business expands, and you may eventually want to open a business location with a showroom full of samples.

It is also a good idea to practice what you preach and use specialty advertising to promote your own business. The simplest way to do this is to have an inexpensive specialty item imprinted with your business name, personal name, and phone number that you hand out in place of a business card during sales calls.

Because your customers are primarily businesses and organizations, newspaper and television advertising is not that effective. You should list your business in the *Yellow Pages*, and consider direct mail advertising. But, for the most part, promoting your business will consist of calling on potential customers both on the phone and in person. Before you begin contacting customers, consider who they are. Some prime customers for specialties are manufacturers, retailers, banks, politicians, and non-profit groups. Find out about your potential customers' needs and problems before you call on them. For example, if you know they are building a new location, you can approach them with ideas on promoting the grand opening.

A virtually unlimited supply of customers are out there, and if you sell them ideas and programs that increase the value of the ad specialty products, they will return to pay for your help.

Getting started as a specialty distributor is inexpensive, but it isn't easy. It takes hard work, lots of energy, and creativity. But if you love to sell, and love to make money, the specialty advertising field can be extremely rewarding.

Companies to Get You Started

To make it as easy for you as possible to get started in specialty advertising, several companies have put together start-up kits consisting of equipment and supplies:

Badge-A-Minit. Create custom buttons with this company's hand-operated press. For $29.95 you can get their Starter Kit which includes the hand press, color-coded assembly rings, ten pre-printed color designs, enough badge parts to make ten buttons, and complete instructions. For $54.95 you can get the Master Kit which includes all of the above, except it has enough designs and parts for fifty buttons, and the Cut-A-Circle device that allows you to cut perfect circles every time. Badge-A-Minit, 348 North 30th Rd., Box 800, LaSalle, IL 61301; 1-800-223-4103.

BASCO. Business Advertising Specialties Corp. With this company's table-top imprinting machine, you can print virtually any message or logo on any item of plastic, metal, leather, wood, ceramic, or glass—flat, curved, or irregular surfaces. They offer a catalog mail distribution program. Free literature, or send $5 for fact-filled video. BASCO, 9351 De-Soto Ave., Chatsworth, CA 91311-4948.

Gold Magic. This company makes an affordable hot foil printing machine with which you can custom-imprint business cards, pens, pencils, match books, award ribbons, binders, photographs, and more. Free information. Gold Magic, Magic Systems, P.O. Box 24986, Tampa, FL 33623.

Mr. Button. The all-metal button-making system offered by this company lets you make custom buttons of two different sizes—2-1/3" and 3-1/8". The press and two dies are $159.95. Mr. Button, Box 68355, Indianapolis, IN 46268.

Polaroid Instant Promotional Photography. With this famous company's special new camera and accessories, you can create all kinds of photo buttons for fund raisers, reunions, sporting events, and more. For just $299 you can get the complete PhotoMagic Kit, including camera and enough supplies to make twenty buttons. Or send for a free video and information kit. NCM Enterprises, Box 165447, Irving, TX 75016; 1-800-678-8014.

Talking Balloons. If you're looking for an innovative specialty advertising product, this is it. These balloons have a computer-generated plastic ribbon. When you slide your thumbnail down the ribbon, the balloon "talks." Many pre-recorded messages are available, but the ribbons can be custom recorded to say almost anything, making them ideal as an advertising tool. Contact: Talking Balloons Inc., 1-800-328-2551.

Denise Osburn

STAINED GLASS

"I really didn't know much about stained glass, only what I'd seen in gift shops," says Hal Williams, owner of Eagle Mountain Stained Glass Studio in Ridgecrest, California. So it was back in 1976, with "zero artistic background" that Williams and his wife Mary decided to take a class on stained glass at the community college. Soon they became good friends with their instructor who owned a stained glass studio. By the end of the year, Williams was hired on at the studio as an apprentice. He stayed there for the next two years, learning most of what he would need to know to start his own business. Williams started a large studio at his home and worked out of it for quite a long time. He gained more experience and training by attending various seminars and workshops around the country.

"All I had was the bare necessities—my hand tools and a bench," says Williams. Eventually, for about $100 Williams purchased a glass grinder used to grind the glass down for precision fitting. Next, he bought a diamond band saw for about $700. This is used for tricky cutting such as 90-degree angles and cutting that cannot be done by hand—it gives the glass worker a professional cut. To round out his studio, Williams bought a glass kiln for $2,000. The kiln is used for glass painting and fusing. It is a necessity when one is restoring the windows of old churches, which Williams has done. "Most of these tools are not necessary when just starting out, but they do save a lot of time for the professional," says Williams.

Initially, Williams made a large purchase of glass, lead, solder, and other supplies because he felt it was necessary to keep these supplies on hand and ready. Since Williams was making so many time-consuming trips to Los Angeles for his materials, he decided to purchase a month's supply at a time. A month's worth of supplies costs him between $1,000 and $1,500.

Other essentials for Williams' office include a work table (which he built himself for under $100) and a bench equipped with a built-in light to trace patterns onto the stained glass pieces.

What It Costs to Start

"Taking everything into consideration, if you are really creative, you can start up for about $2,000," says Williams. "That is if you start up in a home studio." When you are building the stained glass business from scratch, one of the first things you should do is check your competition. This will tell you exactly what supplies to carry. It is obvious that if you don't have a wide palette of colored glass to choose from, you will lose your business to the guy that does.

If you do have competition, be sure there's enough consumer interest to justify your new business. To attract customers to your shop and widen your customer base, offer to teach what you know. Williams went to the local college to offer his skills in stained glass, which they cordially accepted. He is licensed and now teaches twenty-five students a semester.

He also approached local housing contractors and explained that not only could he provide excellently crafted stained glass, but he could also install it and do any necessary repairs on the job. This appealed to them because it would save a considerable amount of money. Their first contract was for stained glass work on twenty-five new houses. Williams created stained glass for front doors and sidelights. Popular colors are various hues of blue, mauve, and desert shades for floral, animal, or desert scenes. He has also done some three- and four-foot windows, and some as large as eight feet.

Williams has a regular business license to do stained glass work, but if you also do the installation work yourself you must have a contractor's license.

Getting the Job

"Proper bidding, I think, is very important in stained glass," says Williams. "If you underbid, you are going to eat it, and if you overbid you are going to lose the job." Williams started out bidding very low so he could get the jobs and prove himself. As time went on he raised his prices, but he is still lower than his competitors. Now he is well known in his area, and gets a lot of good jobs. His biggest job to date was the restoration of all the stained glass in a local church.

Williams makes approximately $3,000 a month on custom work and the sales of supplies, a figure which does not include his contract work and teaching. Williams also has a gift shop in his downtown studio. "To make a decent wage you have to charge a decent price," says Williams. "That's why we added on the gift shop to balance things out."

Spreading the Word

Williams has tried radio and newspaper, but finds that he gets the best results from the local swap sheet. He also carries a large ad in the *Yellow Pages*. Word of mouth has also been a very important advertising factor. Williams has built an excellent reputation and guarantees all of his work. He gets few complaints and generally leaves his customers with smiles on their faces. Williams deals with problems by trying to resolve them as quickly as possible.

Williams strives to keep his customers happy. He tries to understand each client's individual needs and wants. "Some people don't know what they want, so we show them the pattern books. This allows them to visualize their project, whether it's a flower, a tree, or an animal," said Williams. Mary designs what the customer requests and offers them three different sketches. If the customer chooses one, then Williams draws it to scale and starts to build it.

Jo Ann M. Unger

SWAP SHEET

The Swap Sheet is a free classified ads paper that originated in the California Mojave Desert community of Ridgecrest, and is believed to be the oldest continuously operating "shopper" in the entire state. Owner Marie Lint acquired Ridgecrest's Swap Sheet over fifteen years ago when her husband bought the business. However, the bulk of the work was done by the first owner, a young mother named Polly Nicol. Nicol realized there was a real need for a shopper in Ridgecrest because there wasn't a newspaper in the whole city that stores could advertise their goods in. Merchants were intrigued with the idea of a shopper, but familiarizing the townspeople with the idea was a little more difficult. Nicol won the support of the community by going door-to-door, a time-consuming task, but one that apparently paid off. The Swap Sheet has grown in the past fifty years from a circulation of 6,000 to 14,000, and from six pages to forty-four pages. The paper had to be moved from the table-top mimeograph in Nicol's home to an offset press in a downtown office.

Basic Equipment

The first thing that everyone notices about Ridgecrest's Swap Sheet is the color. It is green, and in fact, some people call it the green sheet. Nevertheless, the Swap Sheet is a very attractive paper. Because of its content it is easy to read, and it has been proven effective. The Swap Sheet is free to whoever comes in and picks it up—there is no delivery. Also, there are no salesmen used to sell advertising. Since the paper comes out every Friday it is easy for each merchant to make arrangements for their own advertising.

Whether you are interested in starting your own shopper or taking one over as Lint did, it is very inexpensive. At first, Lint bought larger presses and continued printing the Swap Sheet in the office for quite a few years. Now, it is printed at the large daily newspaper in town. The typesetting machine that is used to produce the Swap Sheet costs about $10,000, according to Lint. She doesn't have paper costs except for the layout boards used for pasting-up the ads. To produce the paper each week it costs somewhere between $1,000 to $1,500, according to Lint. However, she warns that the business changes very quickly, so the price will vary for materials and equipment. "The expense for materials and layout are minor in comparison to the cost for labor and printing," says Lint. For someone just starting from scratch it is still inexpensive.

Using a typewriter and copier at home will suffice until a typesetter and more upgraded equipment can be purchased.

Profits to Be Made

In newspapers the column width is 2", but the columns in the Swap Sheet are 4", 6", 8", and 10". Ads are charged by the height. Contracts are not made, and a discount isn't given if an ad is continuously run. Yet, the price is kept as low as possible.

When Lint bought the business, one of the changes she made was categorizing all of the ads into sections. For example, if a person was looking for a car part they would go right to the car section. Another change that Lint made with the swapper was the price of the ad according to what page it was on. "Everyone wanted to be on the front page or the back page," says Lint. So she decided to raise the price on any "up" page such as pages 3, 5, and 7. She is booked solid for ads on the front and back page through the end of the year. So, advertisers know that they have to reserve a space in advance if they want an "up" page.

An office is now being opened in the nearby mountain community of Kernville. A mass mailing is being done to acquaint the public there with the Swap Sheet. Most of the residents and business owners are aware of the paper's popularity in the county, and this will give them the opportunity to take advantage of the service.

Newspapers don't compete with a shopper. The idea sells itself because when people pick up a shopper they are looking for something specific that they didn't find in the local newspaper. They pick up the Swap Sheet for one reason—to read ads. Many times readers will find what they are looking for which they would not have found any other way. Also, people looking for a specific item will pay to have it listed in the "wanted" section. Plus, if merchants are aware that the public is reading the paper then they will advertise.

Don't let a lack of financing and experience hold you back from creating a swap sheet. The swap sheet doesn't have to have a professional look hot-off-the-presses as long as it is effective. Once the word gets out about the advertising potential of a swap sheet merchants and readers will be clamoring to place advertisements and those advertising dollars will be yours. Do your town, your neighbors, and yourself a service by creating a swap sheet in your community.

Jo Ann M. Unger

Part Five:

12 SERVICE-BASED HOME BUSINESSES

BED & BREAKFAST

Silvia Shepard says she will never forget the visit from the couple who had emigrated recently from Russia. Her family lingered for hours after breakfast, fascinated by stories of their country. The Russia she knew from history books and travel folders came alive with her guests' tales of their lives. Here was a transplanted bit of Russia in her dining room.

She learned from her British guests the proper way of brewing tea. Japanese guests taught her the ancient art of Origami, and she was given the latest news on terrorism and counter terrorism in Israel by a visiting doctor from Tel Aviv. In short, the world drops by to sample your eggs and toast when you have a bed-and-breakfast operation in your home. Not only do you learn about other parts of the world and the USA, but you find yourself using untested skills and discovering intrinsic rewards.

Running a B&B is a creative process. Suddenly, you can be an artist and writer who designs and writes your own brochure, an avant-garde cook experimenting with new dishes, a counselor to a stressed-out guest, an entertainer who sings a duet in Japanese with a guitar-playing visitor from Osaka.

On top of it all you actually get paid well.

How to Get Started

Choose a name. Try to pick one that conveys the feeling of your house or sets a mood, while at the same time reinforcing the best characteristics of your establishment.

It should also be a combination of words that anybody, whether English is their first or second language, can easily relate to. If, for instance, you decide to call your establishment The Keating House, only the people in your town are likely to know who Keating is. Shepard chose Elegant Escape Bed and Breakfast because she wanted to appeal to people who might like to escape to an elegant house.

Determine the price. The rate you charge usually depends on the location and amenities available. If you are in a town with a strong tourist economy, you will be able to ask top dollar. The type of breakfast you offer may determine the price you charge. Thus, you may want to have a two-tier system: one that includes full breakfast for the hearty eaters, and one with a continental menu (orange juice, coffee, and doughnut or Danish). Your price also depends on whether the room includes a private bath. A room with private bath is always more appealing to guests, and commands a higher price.

If your house has an unusual decor, that could be a strong attraction for guests. One bed-and-breakfast operator has a collection of antique dolls and wooden figures handcrafted by her husband. At Christmas the house comes alive with toy soldiers and elves peering through the furniture, while twelve reindeer and Santa in a sled descend from the fireplace. If you have an engaging hobby, display it. You may even want to offer a "mini class" about your particular hobby, telling your guests how you got into it, how easy it is to do, and why you like it so much.

Taxes. In many communities you may be required to collect a "bed tax." In some areas it is officially called the

Transient Occupancy Tax or TOT. The amount varies from city to city.

   Zoning regulations. Such statutes fail to recognize the difference between commercial inns. Let's clear up the confusion:

- *Traditional B&B's.* Most existing bed and breakfasts— sometimes called homestays—usually function in a private home with very little effect on the neighborhood. The hosts live on the premises and have from one to three rooms available for rent. Usually, there is only one group of guests occupying the house, one additional car is parked on the street, and there is very little disruption to the community. The main use of the house is as a private residence. Most B&Bs are traditional.

- *Commercial inns.* These establishments are operated primarily as a business. The owners don't live on the premises, and there are usually four or more rooms available for guests. Several cars are parked in the driveway or on the street and there is a sign advertising the business.

   Insurance. The best insurance available is through the American Bed and Breakfast Association (address below) which has a modest membership fee. A note of caution— there have been reports of homeowners' insurance being canceled when a house is changed to a bed and breakfast. The American Bed and Breakfast Association can advise you on this.

   Brochures and business cards. It is crucial that they provide not only information, but portray the mood you are trying to create. Be sure you mention the rate of the local bed tax, and don't forget to include a map and directions to the house. By having one panel of the brochure contain your name and address, a place for a stamp and room for a return address, you can mail it without an envelope.

Marketing

Join your community's Visitors Bureau. The San Diego Convention and Visitors Bureau, for example, is very active, and publishes quarterly accommodations brochures that are distributed widely in the United States and abroad. The bureau also has visitor booths in several locations, each stocked with information for tourists.

You can buy advertisements in a number of publications, including the *Yellow Pages*, but one of the best sources for B&B customers is word of mouth. Your happy guests are your best advertisement. Always suggest to your guests that they may want to recommend you to their friends. You should leave brochures in the rooms and by the front door so your guests can take them when they go home.

Finally, the American Bed and Breakfast Association publishes a yearly guide called *A Treasury of Bed and Breakfasts*, which lists members' establishments.

Telephone Selling Techniques. Most B&B bookings are made over the telephone, so it is important to have a good telephone presentation. Write out a short paragraph and memorize it. Include the name of your B&B, a short description of the accommodations, and the rates. List your strong selling points first, and stress them. Start by asking the caller, "Is this your first visit to this area?" Then begin selling the town. Mention how lovely the weather is and name the principal local attractions. If the person still cannot decide, say that you would love to have them and that you might be booked next time they call. If they still waver, offer to hold the room for them until the same time next day.

Keep in mind that much of the charm of a B&B is in personal touches: homemade jelly, fresh fruit picked from the garden, and banana bread just like grandma used to make. If you have an old family recipe for muffins or special breads, now is the time to brag about it.

If you have a client who is undecided about whether to book a room or not, you can usually manage to clinch the deal when you get to the part: "and a full breakfast includes eggs Benedict or your choice of eggs, a basket of breads, fruit and juice." After you have made your presentation, use the basic sales technique of asking for the order: "What days can I reserve for you?"

Booking the Reservation

You will need the following information:

1. Name, address, and two telephone numbers (work and home).

2. Dates and type of accommodations. Make sure at this point that you get the correct dates, for example, a reservation beginning on the night of the 10th and going through the night of the 15th.

3. Breakfast preference. Now is the time to give

the personal touch by inquiring about their favorite menus. Some people may prefer a bowl of oatmeal, others a dish of granola. Also find out if they like regular coffee or decaffeinated.

4. Time of arrival. By learning this information ahead of time, you can greet your guests at the door with a warm smile and welcoming words. If you are unable to be there in person, be sure to make arrangements for someone else (a neighbor or friend) to be the welcoming committee.

5. MasterCard®, American Express®, or Visa® number. While you may not have an arrangement to let the guests charge the room on a credit card, asking for a major credit card number is a way to "nail down" the reservation. When they provide this number the transaction has been concluded and they are committed to renting the room. A credit card number also serves as a guarantee for payment if there is any accidental breakage or damages.

6. Deposit. While you may ask for their credit card number as explained above, don't charge the rent to it. Rather, ask that they send a deposit equal to 50 percent of the total price for long stays (five to seven days) and one night's rate on shorter stays (one to four days).

7. Cancellation policy. Good guidelines are: There will be a $20 processing charge on cancellations made at least seven days before the date of arrival. The full deposit is forfeited if the cancellation is made less than seven days ahead of time.

House Rules

Post a list of house rules in each bedroom. These rules should cover check-in and check-out times, smoking policies, use of the telephone, kitchen, and laundry privileges, radio and TV use, etc.

Breakfast Presentation

Next time you go out for brunch at an expensive restaurant, pay attention to the way the food is presented. The curl of a carrot, a tomato made into a rose, bunches of grapes and a slice of cantaloupe added to the plate give the food an extra dimension. By including these and other little (but important) touches, you give your breakfast a professional look.

Membership in Organizations

As this industry grows, there is a need to present a professional attitude and be informed in all areas of the business. B&B operators need to come together as a group to make their voices heard by local government officials. If there is a professional B&B organization in your area, join it. If not, why not start one?

For More Information

The American Bed and Breakfast Association, Village Green, #203, Crofton, Maryland 21114.

Silvia Shepard

BOOKKEEPING

Pamela J. Baker quit her regular job as a bookkeeper. "I liked my job, but I was tired of the looks I'd get from management if I missed work because one of my children was sick. Plus, after my expenses, I was only clearing an extra $20 a week. I said to my husband, 'This is crazy—it's not worth it,' and I quit."

After a friend asked Baker for bookkeeping assistance with her small antiques business, Baker's husband suggested she start her own service. Baker did just that. Starting with only a calculator and one client, she now has a fully equipped home office and ten clients. Her business grossed $28,000 last year.

Baker's business has grown so quickly that she had to hire part-time help, and has a waiting list of prospective clients. She says, "I never realized how many businesses need the type of business service I offer!" Besides bookkeeping, Baker has expanded her business services to billings, mailings and correspondence, payrolls, collection calls, and preparation of tax forms.

When Baker started her business, she checked with her borough about regulations concerning home-based businesses. Getting the okay from them, she set up an office in her dining room. With her first earnings, Baker purchased a good typewriter, a copy machine, and office furniture at a store that buys and sells used business equipment. "I worked successfully for a year and a half with basic office equipment," she says. "I bought equipment and supplies as I could afford them, and never had to get a business loan."

Baker has since added a complete computer system. "I'm lucky because my husband is a computer programmer. He picked out a basic computer for me and showed me how to use a Peachtree bookkeeping program," she says. "At first, some of my clients resisted putting their businesses on the computer, but when I told them it would save them money because it took me less time to do their work, they agreed. Now these same owners depend on my weekly reports of their cash flow. My customers have the advantage of a computerized system without having to own a computer."

Finding Clients

Baker gets most of her clients through word-of-mouth referrals from satisfied clients, and from both a business system salesman and a local tax accountant. "I recommend my customers use Safeguard Business Bookkeeping Systems, because I knew from my own work experience how easy it was to use. Basic packages start at only $60. The salesman who sold me this system now recommends my services to his customers. He also helped me set up my business using this same system," Baker says.

A local tax accountant refers Baker's business to his patrons because it makes his job much easier. "He says having me do his customers' bookkeeping is like having a full-time employee, but without having to pay for one," Baker says.

Who are the businesses that use Baker's services? She says it is mostly the small businesses that gross between $100,000 and $500,000 a year. Baker says, "Generally, these business owners are good at what they do, but not with their books. They might 'rope' their wives into this job, or try to do bills in the evening when they are tired from a full day of work. More often than not, neither is the ideal solution, and the wives are only too happy to have me do this job."

Baker says many of the businesses who use her services are seasonal and do not have enough year-round work to warrant hiring a part-time bookkeeper. "This works out great for me, because usually when one business is slow, another is busy. This allows me to devote more hours to whichever business needs my services the most at that particular time."

When Baker receives a new business referral, she makes an appointment for a consultation for which she charges $30. She hands the prospective client a one-page resumé-type sheet which lists her business services (including her husband's computer consultation services); her training, background, and work experience; her office equipment, including her fax number; and her current rates.

The first thing Baker does when she is hired is to analyze the client's present bookkeeping system. Businesses are often pleasantly surprised, too, after Baker starts doing their bookkeeping. "I have found money for many of my clients. Because of sloppy bookkeeping, deposits are sometimes not entered. I have found as much as $800 to $1,200, and for one client, I found $4,000. Before I took over, the owners of this business thought they were going to have to get a loan for some equipment. With their found money, they did not need the loan."

Earnings

Baker works fifty to sixty hours a week, averaging about ten hours of work for each weekly client, and three to four hours for monthly clients. Approximately twenty hours are spent at the business offices, and the rest are spent in her home office. She charges $12 an hour for her services.

Baker likes to leave Mondays open for appointments, or to work extra hours if she missed a day the previous week. "From the start, I tell my clients that if I take off a scheduled workday to help on a school field trip or because one of my children is sick, I will make up the time the following Monday. In turn, I'll help them out if they should suddenly need me on a Saturday morning or some other unscheduled time. My family comes first, which is one of the main reasons I started this business from my home."

Baker loves doing business from her home, but it has its disadvantages, too. "When your business is in your home you're never closed and you can get business calls at all hours." Baker also says she wants to remodel her garage and make it into a new office. "I'd like my office moved to where I can shut a door on it at the end of the day. It's in the dining room now, and whenever I walk by it, I'm reminded of work."

Baker offers some tips. "Be honest with your clients. Your clients will not trust you if you say you know how to do something and you really don't. I tell my clients if I do not know a procedure, I will find the right person who does. You don't have to know how to do everything, but you do have to know what resources can help you and your client."

For More Information—Home Study Courses

International Correspondence Schools, 925 Oak Street, Scranton, PA 18515. Career Diploma Program in Bookkeeping.

NRI Schools, McGraw-Hill Continuing Education Center, 4401 Connecticut Ave., Washington, D.C. 20008. Home study course in Bookkeeping.

Priscilla Y. Huff

DESKTOP PUBLISHING

Until just a few years ago, businesses, organizations, churches—virtually everybody who circulates information on paper—had two choices: either spend a lot of time designing a publication in-house and taking it to an expensive typesetter, or engage the services of an expensive advertising firm. Today there is a third choice—desktop publishing.

Desktop publishing (DTP) has taken word processing one step further. A computer with the right software and a laser printer can make every document look as though it was produced by a typesetter. With desktop publishing's ability to merge graphics, shading, and various fonts onto the same page with a minimum of cutting and pasting, the typewritten page will soon be considered unprofessional.

Many larger businesses have established their own desktop publishing departments. Now, not only do businesses seek employees with word processing skills, but they also want people who are familiar with page layout software. The competition among businesses to produce highly professional-looking documents can turn your home computer into a gold mine.

Who Needs This Service?

The possibilities are nearly limitless. As mentioned, many larger businesses already have the service in-house. Some of the documents they produce are letters, flyers, forms, reports, presentations, brochures, newsletters, training manuals, magazines, software documentation, books, catalogs, and so on. As a freelancer, you will produce similar documents for those businesses and organizations that do not have the resources to produce them in-house.

Your clients will include small businesses, hospitals, nonprofit and civic organizations, churches, government agencies, and individuals. An example of a prospective client might be a business with thirty or so employees that wants to publish a monthly newsletter to send to its customers. A company of this size usually does not have an employee it can spare to devote to this kind of project. Hiring somebody to take care of just the newsletter does not make sense, not to mention the cost of the equipment. Here's where you come in.

Your product will include all documents listed above and many others. You'll be surprised at some of the things your clients will come up with. Some of the projects are fun.

Equipment

It's difficult to discuss computers and peripherals in so small a space. The best advice for any system application is, purchase the fastest and the best you can afford. The more sophisticated your equipment, the more you will be capable of, and this says nothing of convenience. With that said, there are many things to consider. If you don't already own a computer, before purchasing one you will want to think about compatibility. For our purpose there are two standards, MS-DOS computers (IBMs and compatibles) and Macintosh. There is a lot of discussion in the computer world about which system is best.

However, you will be dealing mostly with businesses, and the industry standard is still MS-DOS. The ability to swap data disks with your clients will make you much more efficient.

With that in mind, the following discussion of computers, software and peripherals applies mostly to the MS-DOS computers, although some Macintosh specifications are not much different.

Most software on the market today, though it will run on a PC XT, is designed for the PC AT or 386 machines. This is especially true of desktop publishing programs. Most page layout software packages are very large programs and run better on a high-speed processor. For best results, your machine should have at least a 286, or AT processor. Another near mandatory requirement is a hard drive. It's difficult, and sometimes, depending on your software, impossible to run DTP programs from a duel floppy system.

Software

You will also need a good word processor. There are several out there that are comparable. But, again, you'll want to remember compatibility. Although it is not essential that your word processing software be compatible with your DTP software, it is highly suggested. This feature, the ability to import text directly into one program from another, will save you considerable time. Your word processor should, at the very least, have the ability to import text in and out of ASCII format.

Many of today's word processing software packages—WordPerfect, WordStar, Microsoft Word, to name a few—have some desktop publishing abilities built in. WordPerfect, for example, can import and automatically wrap text around graphics, download and access laser printer softfonts, adjust columns widths, and do many other page layout functions. One of these word processors, however, will not be the only DTP software you will need. But it will, at times, be the only software you will use for certain documents, such as, say, résumés, which do not require a lot of special formatting.

The more work you can do with your word processor, the better. As mentioned, DTP software is slow. Word processors are generally much faster, and anytime you can finish a document with one software program, the job will tend to be easier.

One of your larger investments will be desktop publishing software. Although there are many programs, only a couple meet the industry standard. It is important that you don't skimp here. All page layout programs are not the same. Some do not handle graphics well, while others are limited in their use of professional-looking fonts. A lot of programs claim to be DTP software, but are really nothing more than expensive toys. The important thing is that your software have the ability to produce documents that have a typeset effect, rather than a blocky, computer-generated appearance.

According to Larry Holt, owner of the highly successful Southern California DTP firm Ventura PageMaking Center, you should choose between one of two packages— Aldus' PageMaker, or Xerox's Ventura Publisher. Although both programs have similar abilities, they are quite different. For this reason, if you have the funds, you will benefit from purchasing both programs.

One or the other, however, will serve you adequately. A big difference between these two very versatile page layout programs is in the way they handle larger documents. Of the two, Ventura Publisher is better equipped for laying out books and training manuals. PageMaker, on the other hand, is somewhat easier to use.

A final note on DTP software: There are, no doubt, other excellent DTP programs available. Please be careful.

Laser Printers

For the best results from your DTP software, you should use a laser printer. Most desktop publishing software will drive dot matrix printers, and often the results are passable. But dot matrix printers should be used mostly for producing drafts and straight typing jobs when a typeset appearance is not required.

There are two standards for laser printers: Hewlett Packard LaserJets and compatibles, and Postscript-typeprinters and compatibles. The LaserJet, usually considerably less expensive, will be all you will need for 90 percent of all layout jobs. Postscript offers better graphic and font versatility, which, after you become a more advanced DTP user, you may find yourself wishing you had access to.

Another drawback to the HP LaserJet is that it usually requires cartridges and downloadable softfonts which you must purchase separately; Postscript printers have a variety of fonts built in. Ventura Publisher and PageMaker, however, do come with a couple of basic softfonts. These fonts should meet the requirements for most of your printing jobs.

An argument for the least expensive printer is that almost all HP LaserJet compatibles can be upgraded later to Postscript standard. If you decide to go with the LaserJet, you should make sure that your printer is equipped with at least one full megabyte of memory for downloading fonts and printing graphics. Again, more is better.

As with some of the other equipment discussed, it is not necessary that you invest in a laser printer right away. You may decide to do drafts on a dot matrix. Then, once you've made all the desired adjustments, take the document to a print shop where laser printers are available for public use. Running off final drafts in this manner is not expensive.

Scanners and Graphics Programs

A scanner is a device that operates like a copy machine in that it takes a picture of images on paper. Using software, the scanner then digitizes the image into computer language, so it can be manipulated on the screen and printed on your printer. Scanners are one of many graphics tools available to computers. Though it is not necessary to purchase a scanner when beginning your service, it is something you will want to think about later. In the meantime, print shops and other desktop publishers will scan images for a very nominal fee.

When you do decide to buy a scanner, be sure to do some research. Many scanners require special software and extra memory to function properly. One inexpensive alternative recently introduced is the hand scanner, a device that will digitize smaller images with reasonable quality. These new products work well for logos and other graphics and they come with their own graphics software.

You will need at least one drawing or paint graphics program to create images for your publications. Some mouses (mice?) come with paint programs, as do hand scanners. Any of these programs will meet your earlier needs. As you get more advanced at desktop publishing, you may want to purchase a more advanced drawing program.

Advertising

Like any other business, you will need to advertise. The key to advertising is to reach as many potential customers as possible for the least amount of money. Most of your clients will be local. The best resource for reaching local businesses is the *Yellow Pages*, which is relatively inexpensive and always at your potential client's fingertips. There are several categories you can list your business under. Ventura PageMaking Center has listings under "Printers" and "Desktop Publishers." Desktop publisher William Harrel has a large ad listing all his services under "Writing," and smaller listings under "Advertising" and "Résumés." Some other good advertising opportunities are: service directories in local newspapers, Chamber of Commerce newsletters and functions, mailouts, and word-of-mouth.

Remember that by the nature of the service, you will be in the advertising business. Consider offering to write advertising copy and produce ads in exchange for advertising space in local publications. Harrel has been writing profiles on his local Chamber of Commerce's officers and trustees in exchange for ad space in the newsletter for several years now.

Your Product and Prices

As your business matures, you will develop a portfolio of past projects you can use as samples. Until then, you can develop products for your business—sample ads, newsletters, and brochures—that demonstrate your writing and page layout ability. If you have had anything published, be sure to include tear sheets in your portfolio.

Harrel's portfolio contains a couple of small booklets, several brochures, a few short stories and articles, flyers, newsletters and résumés (résumés are not a lot of fun, but are terrific for making a little pocket change). Always ask your client for several copies of the finished product to use as samples.

Many new clients will often want documents similar to the ones you show them. You will spend less time on projects of a similar nature than on diverse projects; each time you have to learn something new, such as a new software program or how to make the one you've been using do something different, you will need more time to complete a project.

Pricing your services will be among the more difficult of your decisions. If you bid too much you might scare your customer away; too little will make them wonder about your ability. Try to give estimates based on an hourly rate, such as $25 an hour.

As you gain experience, you will know approximately how long a project should take and how much to charge. As your skills improve and you become more sure of yourself, you can raise your rates. You may at first underestimate how long it would take to complete a project. But you can't expect a client to pay for your inexperience, and you should be prepared to do some jobs over, sometimes more than once. Use the price list in the back of a popular writers' marketing book as a guide for estimating straight writing and editing projects. But you'll be surprised how often you will benefit from having the equipment and know-how to do projects beyond the scope of the conventional writer-editor.

Consider making arrangements with a print shop and a mailing service (many offer discounts to desktop publishers, which you can mark up), so you can offer a more complete service to your clients. Many business people prefer to turn the production and distribution of mailout material over to somebody else, simply because it takes time to run a business.

It will take time for you to run your business. As you get better at writing, editing, and desktop publishing, you will enjoy the challenge of producing professional documents. The best advantage to operating this type of business is that if you learn and continue to grow in your ability both as a writer-publisher and a business person, there is almost no end to the level of success you can achieve.

William Harrel

ENTERTAINMENT SERVICE

Only a few years ago, it was not unusual for Naomi Kolstein to be seen crawling on the floor with a group of youngsters or toting heavy animal carrying cases to birthday parties. For ten years, she was popular at schools and day camps throughout Spring Valley, New York, where she works as the Creature Teacher. With members of her barnyard menagerie that included a goat, she was in demand as the Goat Lady by mothers eager to hold fun-filled parties for their children. However, today Kolstein heads a successful talent agency that provides entertainment for an average of ten parties a week—large and small, corporate and private.

With $500, and a wealth of energy and enthusiasm, Naomi formed World of Entertainment. However, even though Kolstein already was familiar with the ins and outs of the entertainment business she did not neglect to do her homework before launching her newest venture.

Preliminary Research

The preliminaries required five steps that included

advertising, publicity, supplies, attracting entertainers, and finding clients. The preparation period began with lengthy discussions with her husband, an advertising salesman who helped her write efficient ad copy for new talent and clients. Her parents, long-time public relations professionals, gave her assistance with developing promotional techniques such as: making contact with clients in a personal manner; sending out evaluations of her entertainers as a follow-up; reading, investigating, and following up on possible talent and descriptions of events that have already taken place. It was also her parents' suggestion to keep following up to make absolutely sure that not only were performers in the right place at the right time, but that they knew exactly where they were supposed to be, who their audience would be, and the setting that they would be working in.

Next Kolstein went to the local stationery store where she invested approximately $50 in supplies such as binders, 3" x 5" index cards, file folders, push pins, and pens. At this time she also bought $100 worth of postage stamps.

Finding Talent

To build the all-important roster of entertainers, Kolstein began by scouring advertisements in local newspapers and magazines, and by telephoning libraries, schools, cultural centers, camps and Y's. She placed her own ads in local newspapers to recruit types of entertainers she hadn't already discovered. When the family attends fairs, concerts, parties, and other events, it has become routine for them to evaluate the performers and pursue those that measure up to their criteria. Kolstein also always carries a generous supply of business cards to give to possible clients and to performers she thinks may be effective with Naomi's World of Entertainment. As the performers show interest in Naomi's World of Entertainment, their résumés are painstakingly checked and she holds auditions in her office or watches them in action elsewhere.

Naomi's World of Entertainment also maintains rules for the performers. They are not permitted to give their telephone numbers to party hosts or guests. They are not permitted to smoke. They must be prompt. They also must check in with Kolstein within twenty-four hours after an assignment. It is Kolstein's responsibility to confirm all talent and ensure that the performers are top quality.

Performers are the products of Naomi's World of Entertainment and Kolstein is convinced it will continue to thrive only if she maintains the quality and variety of the performers on her roster. When, for example, she is in New York City and notices a mime, violinist, or juggler performing on the sidewalk, she will stop and talk with the person. The casual audition and brief conversation give her an idea of the quality of the person's performance and how the performer relates to the public. At the same time, she is able to observe if the performer is neatly dressed, whether he or she seems to be a responsible person with a positive personality who, for example, can be depended upon to distribute her business cards at parties rather than his or her own.

Finding Clients

Attracting party-givers to her agency was a more complicated procedure. Kolstein already had a list of the names and addresses of the people who had engaged her as the Goat Lady or Creature Teacher. But based on the more sophisticated service she planned to offer, it was necessary to expand and vary the list. To do this, she sent letters printed on her new letterhead stationery that explained the venture to former clients and to schools, shopping centers, libraries, camps, and public centers of every type. She visited party supply shops, caterers, hotel banquet managers and costume renters to personally introduce her agency. Advertising the new business was limited to only one local suburban weekly newspaper with a circulation concentrated in high-income areas.

Adding new party-givers and new talent is a never-ending aspect of the business. Kolstein is unable to devote the hours needed to aggressively seek out possible party-givers. Instead, she relies on contacts she has already made, advertisements in two local newspapers and word-of-mouth recommendations that include hosts who have used performers provided by her agency. Kolstein must be doing a lot that is right. Naomi's World of Entertainment is showing a profit and enjoying a steady rate of growth.

Naomi's World of Entertainment is headquartered in a room set aside in Kolstein's home where, in less than a year, the walls are already covered with performers' business cards, blurbs, brochures, and promotional pieces about the entertainers and the agency. Two fully packed file cabinets hold information about the entertainers. One is reserved for adult event performers and the other for children's entertainers.

Pay Attention to Details

Although the parties are carefree fun, Naomi's World of Entertainment is a serious, efficiently operated business with few, if any, details overlooked. Kolstein regards her phone bill as her major expense which averages out to be about $600 a month. Contracts for the performers and for the clients are a routine procedure for every booking. In addition to stating such expected information as date, place, and hours, the legally worded printed contracts are designed to protect the client, the performer, and Kolstein.

Performers' fees, which begin at approximately $125 and go up to approximately $3,000, are included in the client's bill together with the fee for agency services. Payment time varies. Hosts of large parties pay a 50 percent deposit and send the balance through the mail immediately after the event. Children's party-givers are asked to mail a deposit and give the balance to the performer at the party. "I am very sensitive to the financial needs of the performers," says Kolstein. "I pay them promptly. I am told this is a practice that is seldom adhered to in this business."

To be sure that all has been satisfactory and to learn where any changes may be necessary, Kolstein attends the first party at which an entertainer appears and sends an evaluation questionnaire to every client. The four questions on the evaluation form are geared to the entertainer's overall performance beginning with whether or not he or she arrived on time and ending with whether the host would recommend Naomi's World of Entertainment to others. There is also room for comments.

Today, Naomi's World of Entertainment is able to provide a choice from over 200 entertainers that range from a DJ and ventriloquist to comics, a trained dog act, Dixieland bands and magicians. For a recent corporate party, for example, which was Kolstein's most lavish booking to date, she had two bands, a classical harpist, a magician, two mimes, a ventriloquist, a human statue, and a unicyclist fire juggler. Her most modest booking featured her nine-year-old son, dressed as an elf, greeting Santa and wishing customers a happy shopping experience at a suburban shopping center. Bookings can come from anywhere. A few months ago, for instance, tips from one of Kolstein's young sons brought contracts for a puppet troupe and for a hurdy-gurdy man.

Who is the best candidate to do as Kolstein is doing? Kolstein believes that he or she must be a "high-energy person who truly enjoys a variety of entertainment styles." It is also necessary to love selling. "It is not enough that I like the entertainers, it is essential for me to convey my enthusiasm to clients," says Kolstein. Much of this is done on the telephone. "An agent must also be bold and feel secure enough to set prices without being afraid of scaring off potential clients," says Kolstein. Another aspect to consider before becoming involved in the entertainment business, especially if it will be home-based, is that performers tend to keep unusual hours. "People call here at all hours of the night, and sometimes, at seven in the morning," says Kolstein.

Midlred Jailer

FREELANCE RESEARCH

Today, thousands of Americans are making money by working as freelance researchers. One such person is Bob Rothman, who confides he's making $100 and sometimes even $125 a day in his spare time doing simple research work. "Most corporations and individual businesses don't have the time to put their full-time employees on necessary but time-consuming research projects," says Rothman.

Usually company employees will do their own research, but since it could take hours, it is usually more costly in terms of salary, overhead, and lost time from the job to assign the job to a regular employee. In addition, since many companies are not replacing employees who quit or are paring down their staff, tying up an employee with research could be detrimental to the office work flow.

How to Start

"You need nothing but time," says Rothman. All the research will be done among sources either supplied by your client or readily available at the library. The only thing you really need is the ability to quickly and accurately find material and enjoy digging out details. The following are typical assignments Rothman—and you—would tackle:

- A manufacturer needs all the names of sales managers of certain types in a general area. Rothman looks them up in a commercial directory.

- The marketing division of the local telephone company

needs lists of new home owners in the area. A visit to the local realtor brings results.

- A small advertising agency seeks more business and is looking for new prospective business clients opening up in the area. For this assignment Rothman advises that you visit your city or county records department (licenses and inspection) which will provide names of all individuals involved within the company.

Finding Customers

There are plenty of potential sources for finding clients: letter and mailing shops, retail stores, local manufacturers, fundraising organizations, and advertising agencies— generally, any type of business that seeks specialized customers. "All you have to do," says Rothman, "is to get a paper and pen and go to your phone book and local library to get a complete list of every business that fits into these categories." Write to your prospects outlining your services (you are a custom research business that is able to collect and record information on a wide variety of topics).

Rothman stresses that you should send a letter of introduction and samples of your work to each and every business that you feel might possibly use your service. "When I first started out," he says, "I was always hesitant to send material to either really big or really small companies because I thought there was no way I could get them as clients. That's a negative attitude that I know cost me thousands of dollars."

Once you've written to the companies, follow up with a phone call a week later. Try at this point to get a personal interview. This is not the kind of service that can be sold immediately with a single letter or phone call. All you want to do is establish a line of communication with someone important. Then, when a job comes up you'll be the first one he thinks of. "The best way to grow in this business is to work hard to add more clients, and always be on the lookout for people who can recommend you to others," says Rothman.

Advertising and Earnings

Word of mouth is your best form of advertising. Companies keep up with what other companies are doing, and if you develop a reputation as a good researcher, you could build a client list.

What can you earn? Rothman always charges by the actual time it took him to do the job. It's not unusual to ask for and receive $6 to $8 an hour for even simple work. "This is the kind of business that you can really start out with nothing and slowly build into a money-maker that will last for years," says Rothman.

Louis Epstein

NEW AGE SERVICES

What is the "New Age"? To most people, the term "New Age" may be incomprehensible, but a great deal of it is very practical and applicable to everyone's life. New Age encompasses everything from holistic healing and health foods to subliminal tapes and meditation. Some of the more exotic areas of New Age touch on the occult and channeling spirits. Most of these beliefs, ways of thinking or living, and products are old ideas—some millennia old—simply resurrected in a world changing faster than many people realize.

Believe in them or not, the many facets of the New Age are an ever-increasing trend that shows little sign of stopping. Millions of people subscribe to one idea or another of the New Age. More importantly, people are spending a great deal of money on their beliefs—which means you can profit. A great number of New Age practitioners, as well as open-minded entrepreneurs, have parlayed their beliefs and opportunities into profitable businesses.

Some reading this might think that the chances of starting a successful New Age business are very slim. Those people would be wrong because, though there are no statistics, a conservative estimate would put 75 percent of the U.S. population agreeing with at least one aspect of the New Age. That's a lot of people looking for services.

Finding a New Age business idea is as difficult as any other business, but no more so. The success of your business will depend on the number of interested people in your community, but mail order is also a very good opportunity. To start a New Age business, you will have to become familiar with the scope of New Age ideas, no matter what your own beliefs may be.

Most New Age practitioners have their own area of belief and practice, such as practicing Tai Chi and meditation. Others have a more varied approach to these topics, adopting beliefs and skills that are incorporated into their life. Still others want a no-nonsense and practical approach to their own religion (Catholicism, Judaism, etc.).

Much of this background knowledge can be gleaned

from library books or books purchased in your local bookstore. There may also be a New Age society in your community—this can be the best source of contacts and potential clients. You needn't understand or accept any of these ideas, but you should know what is available so you can discuss it intelligently. Be prepared to find that many New Age believers will share beliefs that you have held as truth for many years. UFO phenomena and reincarnation are two of the most popular beliefs, not only in the New Age but in the whole of society.

To help the uninitiated, here is a small list of some of the less-specialized New Age businesses anyone can start:

Graphology

The ability to practice graphology, or handwriting analysis, is not a special gift and does not require any type of supernatural ability. Anyone can learn the basics and make spare-time profits. The key to gaining skill is practice—you have to learn by doing. There are at least three ways to profit:

1. **Mail order.** You can obtain clients by inserting a classified ad in a local newspaper or national magazine. The ad might read: "Handwriting Analysis. Send $10 and handwriting sample to (your name and address)." Clients will mail in a handwriting sample, you will analyze it, and return the analysis to the client. You'll probably find that women's magazines are the best places to advertise. The fee you charge will depend on

the audience the particular magazine reaches; a more upscale magazine reader might be willing to pay $15 to $20.

2. **Personal consultation.** This home-based business has clients bringing you handwriting samples, usually with a particular question in mind. You do the analysis and answer the client's question. Such business is most often generated by word of mouth, but an ad in the *Yellow Pages* and a supply of business cards are helpful in obtaining clients.

3. **Roving analyst.** Take your ability anywhere that attracts a lot of people, such as malls, art festivals, and shopping centers. After paying any required fee, set up a table and a couple of signs. Since you may be analyzing anywhere from fifteen to twenty writing samples an hour, your fee can be low—$2 or $3.

To learn this art, consult these books: *Handwriting Tells* ($9), *Handwriting Analysis Made Easy* ($7), and *What Your Handwriting Reveals* ($5), each available from E.A. Morgan Publishing Co., P.O. Box 1375, Huntington, NY 11743.

Psychic Advice

Robert C., a man from Toronto, Canada, is making money with his $12 mail order "Psychic Profiles." Two to four weeks after buyers send him his filled-out questionnaire (and their money), they get back a fourteen-page profile, including astrology, I Ching, biorhythm, worst times, best times, states of consciousness, and so on. Advertise in publications likely to attract interested customers.

Health Farm

Several years ago, Austrian-born Elza G. began the New Age Health Farm in upstate New York with a week's food and $200 worth of stationery. Now she has a big place in the mountains where her guests benefit from health regimens, as well as her expertise in lay counseling and astrology. She doesn't charge directly for her psychic counseling, but it's an added attraction that makes her place popular.

Paraphernalia

Crystals, pyramids, meditation robes, incense, and other objects and materials related to the New Age could be sold for profits. Mail order and flea markets are two viable methods of making part-time profits.

Dream Analysis

Like graphology (see above), you'll need to learn the art before you can go into business. And once you learn to interpret dreams with authority, you can, as with graphology, offer your services via mail order, as a home consulting business, or at fairs and malls. A helpful book is *How to Understand Your Dreams*, $7 from E.A. Morgan Publishing Co., P.O. Box 1375, Huntington, NY 11743.

Astrology

If you regularly flip to the horoscope section of a newspaper, or buy the periodical astrological forecast guides sold in bookstores, why not turn this interest into personal profit? Even if you're not a follower or a fan, you can take advantage of the popularity of astrology. Since the subject intrigues so many people, you will find prospective clients for individual horoscopes all around you. For less than $50 you can buy virtually all of the materials you need to learn the art of casting and interpreting a horoscope. You must be able to write creatively, have the patience for research, and the ability to master a few mathematical equations. You will be adding, subtracting, and multiplying time in hours, minutes, and seconds. As several conversions are required for each chart, patience for detailed, multi-step work is required for this vocation. You must also be a reference book collector; money for this should come from your profits.

Some other ideas include:

- New Age cosmetics salesperson (anti-aging creams, non-allergenic cosmetics and ozone-friendly products for personal care are popular among New Age enthusiasts).

- Health food store (if your town doesn't have one, this is a guaranteed money-maker, and not just among New Agers).

- Meditation center or workshops (meditation techniques are easy to learn, and a great many people are interested in the calming and stress-reducing effects of light meditation).

- Promoting New Age workshops and seminars in your community (people love workshops/seminars and often enroll just out of curiosity; this could be expanded to include a wide variety of off-beat topics).
- New Age newsletter.

Many of these ideas came out of the classified section of just one New Age publication, *The New Age Journal*, perhaps the greatest New Age resource. The range of services includes everything from gemology to the manufacture of prayer robes. Services are very popular with New Age practitioners. Like most, those entrepreneurs simply saw an opportunity for a business and went for it.

Another word of warning, though. Like many new ideas and many controversial subjects, you have to expect your New Age business to attract criticism. A great many people, particularly people with deep religious convictions, often misunderstand New Age ideas and equate the whole of New Age with the occult, satanism, and perversion—none of which have anything to do with New Age thinking—but the idea does exist in many people's minds, and they do not hesitate to tell others.

Ken Larkman and Perry Wilbur

PET-MO-BILE SERVICE

Most of us have used a taxi at one time or another, especially if you work or live in an urban setting. Janet Jones has her own taxi service, but it isn't for people. Jones' taxi service, Pet-Mo-Bile, is for people's pets. Jones' "passengers" include dogs, cats, rabbits, birds, and some small livestock such as goats and sheep.

Jones charges $10 to $15 for one-way transportation, though rates may vary according to the number of pets the owner wants transported, their size, and the distance involved. Jones has a van equipped with animal crates of various sizes, leashes, and harnesses to insure the safety of the animals while they are in the vehicle. She is having her van painted with the name of her business, so it will be recognizable in the communities she serves.

Jones will deliver the animals for a variety of appointments, such as grooming, veterinary surgery or check-ups, boarding, flea dips, or to any other destination the owner wants. "My service is provided for people without transportation, busy work schedules, or for those who just want to stay in bed," she says. Jones realized there was a need for this service when so many of her friends and family would ask her to take their pets to appointments, because she was available during the day. "People knew I worked at night, and that I could take their pets to appointments," she says.

Jones has worked with various kinds of animals for over fifteen years, giving her experience and knowledge of animal behavior that is invaluable to her in this profession. Because of her experience, one veterinarian wanted to hire her as a veterinary technician. "I was flattered," Jones says, "but I did not want to go back for three years of schooling, which is very expensive. I have fun with animals in my own business."

In addition to her taxi service, Jones also offers an emergency ambulance service for sick or injured animals. "I offer this service, but it's not my favorite part of the business." She explains, "Sometimes I am called when an animal has already died, or the police call me to pick up an animal that has been abused by its owner. That's hard for me to do. I'd rather stick with the happy part of my business—my pet taxi."

Other Services

Aside from the taxi, Jones offers pet owners additional services. She carries various novelty and medical (non-prescription) supplies in her van. She has a varied list of suppliers of these products, and can get most items a pet owner may want. Another part of her business is filling special food orders. Jones says some animals are on special diets, and the owners find it inconvenient to drive to an out-of-the-way place on a regular basis to pick up the food. She charges a pick-up fee, plus so many cents per mile for this service.

Jones will also design special "cat yards" for owners who live in communities where cats cannot roam free. She maintains that cats do not adapt well when fitted with a collar and leash. The yards provide a safe haven for the cats, while insuring their safety. The average price of designing and building these enclosures is approximately $600 to $3,000, depending on the complexity of the yard. She will give free estimates, and can build these structures as small as a square yard or large enough to enclose a cat owner's entire backyard. Jones is extremely handy with tools and does all the construction herself.

Jones sees the future of her business as a full-time enterprise. "It gets a little hectic, especially since I hold a full-time job at night, and run the Pet-Mo-Bile service during the day," Jones says. "I would like to be able to have my van parked on a regular basis at certain locations with pre-announced schedules. For example, I could park across the street from a senior citizens' housing complex at certain times, and they could buy the pet products they need, or have me take their pet to a designated appointment."

Advertising

To advertise her Pet-Mo-Bile, Jones had business cards printed with a cute illustration of a van carrying a dog and cat. She also had flyers printed describing in detail all of the services she offers. Jones says, "I put both cards and flyers in veterinary offices, grooming shops, feed stores, etc., and have had a good response. Good service, of course, helps my business when satisfied customers spread the news by word of mouth."

The main reason Jones has been doing so well is that she loves animals. As she says, "Each animal has a different personality, but there hasn't been one I did not like." Jones' service has proven so useful to pets and their owner, that her Pet-Mo-Bile is sure to keep "rolling along" with plenty of animal passengers for many years.

Priscilla Y. Huff

PET SITTING

CAREER OPPORTUNITIES
Flexible hours. Promising salary. Holidays nego-
tiable. Be your own boss. No experience necessary.

If you spotted the above ad in the Help Wanted section of your local newspaper you might laugh and think it's too good to be true. But it is true. One of the easiest home businesses to start and operate requires very little money. The only necessary skills are patience, time, and lots of love. The business is pet-sitting!

Jackie McDonald, owner of Jackie's Pals, started her pet-sitting business after working eight years in a doctor's office. "I wanted to do something I enjoy," she says. "I love animals and I find this work very calming." McDonald spoke with other pet-sitters in her area and discovered how busy they all were. But she knew her neighborhood could support another pet-sitter.

Pet-sitting involves going into someone's home and caring for a pet when the owner isn't available. The service can include plant watering and mail and newspaper pick-up. The focus, however, is on the animal. Pet-sitting saves the client and the animal the aggravation of dealing with a kennel. Clients expect a variety of services: feeding, watering, litter box cleaning, pill giving, and especially some Tender Loving Care for a lonely animal who misses its master.

Advantages, Disadvantages

Owning a pet-sitting business has many of the same advantages of owning any business—you are your own boss, you set your own hours (depending on the number of clients you serve per day), and your paycheck will be limited only by your willingness for hard work. McDonald especially enjoys the flexible hours. Another advantage of pet-sitting is the opportunity of getting to know some real characters: Missy, the cat who only eats facing north (a real example, believe it or not), or Rufus, the blue-footed Amazon parrot who refuses to stay in a cage. McDonald describes the pleasure she finds in meeting both pets and their owners: "Ninety-nine percent of the people are very nice. Most are concerned about their pets or they wouldn't call me. And the animals love me no matter what."

As with any business, pet-sitting has a few disadvantages as well. If the business is to succeed, long hours and hard work are necessary. "This is not a get-rich-quick scheme," McDonald says. Holidays will be especially busy. Servicing fifteen pets, each two times per day is not an unreasonable expectation. That doesn't leave much time for football viewing on New Year's Day. Unless you're a real animal lover some of the tasks can be unpleasant: Who wants to clean a litter box twice a day for two weeks? But that wildly wagging tail or the purr of a lonely animal that greets you at the door does make it worth the trouble. So do those paychecks at the end of the Christmas holidays. "You must truly love animals," McDonald advises, "or you won't enjoy this business."

Start-Up Costs

Start-up costs for a pet-sitting business are small. Expenses can be divided into three categories: marketing, insurance, and transportation. Initial outlay can be as little as $200 or as much as $300 if you choose to pay for a visit to an accountant. That isn't a bad idea. An accountant can explain tax laws and policies governing this type of business. In some states, for example, he or she will tell you not to charge sales tax because you perform a service that is not taxable.

Although most clients will come your way by word of mouth, invest in a few marketing tools. Business cards are essential. Costing anywhere from $25 to $50, business cards can be placed anywhere pets are found—pet shops and vet clinics. Because most vet clinics have kennel facilities, some may not allow you to place your card with them. Establish a relationship with a vet in your area, though, and he or she will begin to recommend you when the kennel facility is full. Design a flyer and place copies on community bulletin boards, church bulletin boards, at the grocery store, and any other place you can think of. "Welcome-to-the-community" associations may be willing to give your card to new residents, too. Keep trying to get your business known. People will be delighted with this service when they hear of it and hear that you are a top quality pet-sitter. If you can afford it, buy an answering machine. Once your business is booming, you'll need one to take all your business calls.

Clients will ask if you are bonded. This means that an insurance company finds you trustworthy and is willing to put that in writing. An insurance policy protects the homes you enter. If something is broken while you are there, your policy will cover it. Being bonded, however, does not protect against damage to pets while in your care. With this type of policy, your premium increases as your business increases. Initially your coverage could cost $100 per year. As your client list increases, you could pay as much as $500 per year. Being bonded, however, is worth the expense. Clients are more likely to use your service if you're backed by an insurance company.

Keep a log of business miles traveled in your car. Also keep track of gas and other auto expenses. These are all tax deductible.

Operations

When a client calls, arrange a meeting before his departure. This gives you an opportunity to see the pet, familiarize yourself with the routine, and get a key. The client also gets to check you out and give instructions. Appear professional. Have a printed instruction sheet ready for the client to complete. Include space for emergency phone numbers and vet information. Also include a section on pet preferences. A pet whose routine has no disruptions is a much happier one when master returns. The master will be satisfied and you'll reap the benefits by gaining a repeat client.

"Suggest that clients limit changes to a pet's routine," McDonald advises. The pet will be happier and easier to care for. Provide references to all clients who ask. When you're just starting out, ask a neighbor whose cat you've fed once or twice if she'll be a reference. Most clients won't call references, but will be wary if you've got no one to vouch for you. An important note here: ask clients to be specific about when they'll be returning. Have them call you when they do get home. Avoid the disaster of one pet-sitter whose client was three days delayed and whose cat went unfed for that time. When you return your client's key you pick up your payment.

What to Charge

Determining a fee is a personal matter. McDonald consulted other pet-sitters in the area to determine an appropriate charge. Fees range anywhere from $5 to $10 per visit. Some pet-sitters charge more for an initial visit and less for subsequent visits. The fee will also depend on the number of pets involved and the amount of trouble they will be. Obviously the household with three cats, a turtle, two birds, and a hamster should be charged more than the one with a single dog. Decide in advance what your limits are, too. If you don't care to feed, water, and brush a horse each day be prepared to say no. Once your business takes off, one turned down request won't affect you. If you live in a large city, you will have to decide how far you're willing to travel. Consider limiting the area you service or charge more for long-distance visits.

A wide variety of people will use a pet-sitting service. Certainly vacationers will be a number-one market. Therefore, holiday times will be extremely busy. Some people own pets but have little time to spend with them—couples who both work full-time, and singles who travel a great deal. These people can become permanent clients and provide a steady income in non-holiday times.

A few words of advice and notes of caution:

- Be prepared for a mess. Bored animals are messy little things. They knock over plants, break vases, and chew furniture. Although yours is not a house-cleaning service, your clients will appreciate your efforts to tidy things up.

- Follow your client's instructions to the letter. Even if no one but you knows that Fido ate exactly at 6 P.M., do what is asked. Owners can detect when a pet's routine has gone awry.

- Pregnant women should be aware of a condition known as toxoplasmosis. Caused by a parasitic organism found in cat feces, toxoplasmosis can cause severe damage to a fetus. Pregnant women should use extreme caution when disposing of cat feces or else wait until after the baby is born to start a pet-sitting business.

- Expect a few complainers. Most clients will love you. Some, however, will be annoyed that Fifi's nails grew too long while she was in your care, or that Bucky seems listless since their return. Many pets experience depression when separated from their masters. As long as you have done your job well and followed instructions exactly, take complaints with a grain of salt.

A pet-sitting business is an easy one to start. The only requirement is a real love for animals. You will find that people are quite interested in your service and are more than willing to pay for it. McDonald sums it up this way: "This is a very time-consuming business. But I really enjoy it and I've learned from it. You're certainly compensated and it is very satisfying."

For Further Information

Pet Sitting for Profit by Patti J. Moran. Howell Book House, 866 Third Avenue, New York, NY 10022; $14.95.

National Association of Pet Sitters, 1020 Brookstown Ave., Ste. 3, Winston-Salem, NC 27101.

Patricia J. Hazlett

PHOTO AGENT

Mention a home stock-photo business to anyone interested in starting a home business, and chances are good you will get two different responses, one being, "You've got to be kidding," and the other, a blank face. The smart, enterprising soul, after being armed with specific information concerning the photographic marketplace, will realize rather quickly that there is a lot of money to be made.

Here's how it works. Both freelance and professional studio photographers generate images which offer sales potentials from $25 to $500 per purchase. However, seldom do these individuals have the time to market them properly. Here is where your home photographic agency steps into the picture. Acting as a go-between, the home-based agent can sift through the potential markets, query each with a listing of on-file images, and sell the photographs.

Each image sold nets the agent from 30 to 50 percent of the market value. The other portion goes to the photographer. Selling just one photograph per day for an average of $50 nets the agent from $15 to $25. Now, that might not sound like much, but it is only the beginning. Seldom does only one photograph sell for $50. Through the use of one-time rights, an agent can sell the same photograph over and over again. Furthermore, chances are good that more than one photograph will sell to the same publication and at the same time; more typically, from three to five photos will be sold.

It is not uncommon to see checks from $150 to $1,000 enter the mailbox each day. When half of that is the agent's, it's clear that income from agenting photographs is a very lucrative home business.

Finding Markets

Unless you live in New York City where there are many well-established stock photo agencies, you have a very good chance of becoming highly successful at this business. As you progress, you will discover other potential markets for stock images in your area. There are local, regional, and nationwide galleries, interior decorators, and picture rental markets besides the newspapers, commercial and trade publications. Pictures sell to book publishers as well.

The first step to take is to adjust your mental frame of mind. Both freelance and professional studio photographers share a common goal: to become published photographers. However, seldom are they able to fully market their work. They probably know less about marketing their photographs than you have already learned by reading this text. And once you complete this section, you will certainly know more about marketing photographs.

The second step is taken when you purchase the *Photographer's Market* (published by Writer's Digest Books), a book that can be purchased at your local bookstore or found in your library's reference section. It contains your leads.

The third step is to discover what is going to sell and what isn't. How do you do this when you are living in Sulphur, Louisiana, and the markets are all over the world? There are a couple of ways. Drive around your area and look at the natural resources within a fifty-mile radius;

look, too, at the local industry, businesses, and architecture. Another way would be to pull out the *Yellow Pages* phone directory; many stock pictures are based upon civic center events, trade shows, human interest images, and scenics.

You have only spent about $50 so far: $20 went for the market book, the rest was spent on driving around. If your area is typical of many places in this country, by the time you have traveled about and scanned through the *Yellow Pages*, you have already gotten excited about the area's potential.

At this point, however, you need feedback from potential publications. There are over 2,500 publications listed in the *Photographer's Market* book. Now you need photographic guidelines. Get copies of the appropriate publications (at least one, perhaps three back issues) to see what kinds of photos are used. Write to those publications which: (1) state an interest in stock images; (2) will pay the most money; (3) buy the most images from photographers; find out what rights they purchase.

To do this professionally, you need a letterhead and envelopes. You will also need self-addressed envelopes (SASEs) to assure a return reply. Address each letter to the photographic editor and announce that you are a picture agency. Inquire how many stock images are purchased annually without a manuscript. Mention in your letter that the images are going to be from your region. This will filter out publications not interested in such photos.

In doing your research, notice where the bulk of the image requirements lie. You could discover that human interest pictures or scenics are in demand from your area. Whatever the subject, you are going to be armed with the knowledge necessary to gain freelance and studio photographers' attention.

Finding Photographers

You are now ready to capture the attention of local freelance and studio photographers. Place an ad in your local paper like this:

> FREELANCE AND STUDIO PHOTOGRAPHERS
> NEEDED. If you are a freelance photographer or
> a studio pro and have stock images you would like
> agented, please contact: The Ace Photographic
> Agency at 555-1234.

When you are contacted, don't talk business strategy with the photographer over the phone. Rather, tell the photographer that you would like to see him at his convenience at your office with samples of his work. At this meeting, after looking over his work and determining whether or not he has the skills and talent necessary to produce the kinds of images required to sell, suggest the types of photos you need. If you're satisfied with his work, draw up a contract with the photographer that covers your agency's commission.

The photographer should provide you with duplicates of his original photos, not the originals. Find out if the images have ever been published before, and if so, when and where. You need to know what rights were purchased. If all rights were purchased, you can't re-market those images. If first rights only were purchased, second- or one-time rights can be negotiated with other publications.

Write to the publication that bought first rights and confirm the fact that the photos were published and under the first-rights agreement.

Now you are ready to market the photos. To the publications you have chosen, send total packages of images. The average is 200 images in the form of duplicate slides. Send a dozen black-and-white images along with contact sheets of the same amount of negatives. While this might sound costly at first, once this overhead is absorbed, all that is required is a ninety-day cycle of updated lists of stock material.

The mailings will run from $2 to $5 initially. If you are mailing to over 100 publications, you'll invest $200 to $500. But the investment is worth it when those checks begin to arrive.

When publications ask for certain types of photos, you can charge them a research fee of $25 and up. For this they receive from you a dozen or so photos that meet their requirements. When they decide on a photo or photos, negotiate a usage price of between $25 and $500 dollars per image. This variation in price will depend on the size of the image when used, the circulation of the publication, whether it is black and white or color (charge more for color), and where in the publication it will be used (charge more for cover usage).

Strive to work with publications that pay on acceptance first. This will provide you with a cash flow to cover for sending out images to publications that pay on publication. Also, when you contract a photographer, be sure to include cost of overhead as part of the before-profit-is-realized clause. Remember, these photographers would absorb this overhead cost as part of the business of marketing their own images; it is as much a part of their cost as it is yours.

When all of this begins to show profits and the rest of the market possibilities begin to open, you will discover quickly why the home photographic business is one worth your time and effort.

For More Information

Photographer's Market. Writer's Digest Books, 1507 Dana Avenue, Cincinnati, OH 45207; $22.95 ppd.

R.T. Edwards

INCOME TAX PREPARATION

It happens every April—income taxes. Most of us are concerned with refunds or payments when we think about filing our income tax. There are some, however, who look at filing income tax as a great income opportunity year after year.

Preparing income taxes can be very profitable and is easier than you think. Many franchises have cropped up across the country that offer this specialized service, and there are several home study courses that can train you (see below).

Once you have gathered all your information, publications, instructions, and forms (see the list below for what you'll need), you are ready to begin establishing your home business. As with any new business, you need to have the proper state/local licenses. When you contact the state and local tax officials for information, discuss any requirements they may have for new businesses.

Since income tax preparation is seasonal, you will probably want to work on a part-time basis, or as a supplement to an existing business. Remember that the overwhelming majority of your income tax preparation business will be from January through April, although there is other tax preparation business during the year. Some of your clients will receive notices from the IRS throughout the year and will need your assistance in handling these matters. Businesses need certain types of taxes prepared throughout the year. Of course, any extensions you file will have to be prepared by August, and if any clients need amended returns filed, this may be done any time during the year.

You will need an office to work from. A spare room, den, or adequate space in your living area for an office is ideal. Whatever area you choose, make sure it has a professional appearance, adequate furnishings for visiting clients, and a telephone.

If space at home is a problem, you may do business at your client's home or business by picking up their information and returning it to them upon completion. Operating your business outside your home or office can be time consuming, and this may limit the total number of returns that you can prepare. Another alternative is to rent office space, but you must remember this also increases your operating costs.

An alternative to working out of your home is to rent temporary space from another established business. Sometimes a mall, shopping center, or other established business has enough room to sublet you an office area during the tax season. If you choose to sublet your office, make sure your clients know you are available year-round by telephone and by personal visits to their home or office.

Finding Clients

After finding your location and establishing your office, you will need to set your business hours. Your hours should be convenient to you and your clients, and should include days, evenings, and weekends from January through April.

You will need to advertise your business, but don't overdo it. Start small, depending on the volume of business you desire, and the overhead expenses you can afford. Word-of-mouth where you are employed, distributing business cards, and posting and distributing handbills in public areas all seem to work very well. A mailing campaign to friends, neighbors, relatives, and business acquaintances also works well. You might consider offering some incentive in your mailing campaign. Classified advertisements in newspapers or trade papers work well for this type of business.

Now that you are open for business and clients are pouring in, the first thing you must do is interview your client. The most efficient, effective, and least costly way to interview a client is by using Form 1040. Although the client may not need to file this form (he or she may be able to use 1040A or 1040EZ), most information about an individual's tax status can be outlined with the use of the 1040 as an interviewing guideline.

If the taxpayer has brought his IRS tax preparation package, use the label and the pre-addressed envelope from that package, discarding or returning the remainder of the package. After completing this part, interview the client, and question him about each line on the 1040. As you come to a line that requires additional forms or information, stop at that line until you have gotten the additional forms and completed them.

Once you have thoroughly interviewed and questioned the client and calculated his refund or payment, be sure that you complete the "Paid Preparer's Use Only" section of the form. The completion of this section is an IRS requirement. Do not have the taxpayer sign the return. Explain that you will review the return for accuracy, making sure all information and calculations are correct. Tell him that in three to five days (determine a date or say you will telephone) the return will be available for him to pick up. Determine your fee and ask your client if he would like to pay now or when he comes for the return. Make sure you thank the client, and after he has left, file the return so that you can recheck and recalculate it once the office is closed.

The rechecking and recalculating process is very important and care should be taken in reviewing each return. If a discrepancy is found, make sure you telephone your client with the information.

Other helpful hints for your income tax preparation business:

• Don't be afraid to look in your reference material to answer questions. Remember, you are the expert or your client wouldn't be there.

• You must make a photocopy of the return for your files—it is a requirement of the IRS and is handy in preparing next year's return, or if the client needs a copy later in the year.

• Make sure you have a printing calculator at your desk.

• Complete all forms in pencil so that when you recheck the return, mistakes can be easily corrected. Make photocopies to give to the client for filing with the IRS and for his personal records. You should keep the original forms in your file.

• Completed and checked, the return should be assembled with the 1040, 1040A, or 1040EZ. All IRS forms have an attachment sequence number printed in the upper right-hand corner. The sequence number indicates the order in which the forms should be assembled.

• Your client should be given copies of all information that was given to you (you keep copies too). All the photocopied returns and information for the client should be given to him in a folder or envelope.

• Remember to show the client where to sign the return(s) and to date them when they are ready to mail in the envelope(s) that you included from the taxpayer's original package.

What do you charge for this service? Typically, from $25 to several hundred dollars depending on the complexity and time involved. Many accountants and bookkeepers charge by the hour. Keep it simple, yet profitable, by establishing a charge per form.

Begin with a charge for the 1040, 1040A, and 1040EZ, and then determine a fee for preparing each schedule and additional form. Each should have a separate fee for preparation based on its complexity and time for completion.

At the end of your interview, explain the charges to your client, making sure he understands that your fees are not based on the payment or refund, but on the number of forms that are needed to be filed as required by the IRS.

Forms and Information

Lots of basic information is available from your local IRS office, your post office, or your library. Your best and most efficient source of information is the IRS. You should request the following free IRS publications that will prove to be very helpful:

1. *Your Federal Income Tax*, Publication 17. This publication is a detailed reference guide to preparing tax returns for individuals. You will find answers to most of your preparation questions in this publication.

2. *Tax Guide for Small Business*, Publication 334. This publication is a detailed reference guide to preparing tax returns for businesses. You will find the answer to most of your questions on income, excise, and employment taxes for individuals, partnerships, and corporations in this publication.

3. *Information for Tax Practitioners*, Publication 1045. This publication gives you information you need to know as a tax preparer. You can also order forms and publications with the enclosed order form.

4. *Instructions for Form 1040 and Schedules A, B, C, D, E, F, and SE.* A detailed publication giving

you line-by-line instructions for completing these forms. It is a good idea to study this publication in detail before beginning your tax preparation business and then keep it handy as a reference guide.

5. *Instructions for Forms 1040A and 1040EZ.* Also a detailed instruction booklet. This publication gives you line-by-line directions for these forms.

6. *Guide to Free Tax Services,* Publication 910. You should take the time to study this publication. You will find information on free publications, free phone service, free person-to-person assistance, and filing tips.

Remember, the IRS has a publication on most any tax subject and they are usually supplied to you free of charge. If all else fails, you can always call the toll-free tax assistance number for your area and have your question answered.

The backbone of your business is the various forms you will be completing for your client/taxpayers. You can obtain IRS tax forms and publications from the "Forms Distribution Center" for your state or by visiting the IRS office closest to you, or from your local participating bank, post office or library. You may also call the toll-free "Forms Only" number—1-800-424-3676 from 8 A.M. to 5 P.M. Monday through Friday, and on Saturday from 9 A.M. to 3 P.M. during the tax season. If you need just one copy of a form that you will not commonly use, the library has copies of most IRS forms. These forms can be photocopied, usually right at the library.

Computer tax preparation is increasing. Many good software programs exist for computation of individual and business income tax return. Once prepared, the hardware and software necessary to transmit a completed return via modem to the IRS Service Center is very complex and somewhat expensive. Also, electronic filing service from your terminal to the IRS requires a very strict procedure. For details on electronically filing returns with your computer, write the IRS office nearest you and request Publication 1345, *Revenue Procedure for Electronic Filing of Individual Income Tax Returns*. Begin preparing your income tax returns manually, unless you are very familiar with computers and wish to make a large initial investment in hardware and software.

To make your income tax preparation business more profitable, you will also need to prepare state and local income tax forms, if they are required in your area. You should write your state tax department and inform them you are an income tax preparer and you will need their instructions and forms for the current year. It is also a good idea to visit the nearest state tax department field office to get acquainted with the personnel and any services they might provide.

If your local area has an income tax requirement, you will need to gather the necessary instructions and forms for its preparation. It may be best to visit with them in person; they may be able to refer clients to you. Most state and local income tax forms are simple and can be learned quickly. You will use the same information from the Federal forms on the state forms.

An income tax preparation service can prove to be a very profitable and easily operated home-based business.

Remember to gather your information free from the IRS, establish your office and clients, prepare, and check honest, fair, and accurate returns. These professional habits will lead to a profitable business of your own.

Home Study Courses

Federated Tax Service, 2021 W. Montrose Ave., Chicago, IL 60618. Free information.

National Tax Training School, Box 382, Monsey, NY 10952. Free information, plus booklet, *Building a Successful Tax Practice*.

Lee Harbert

TYPING SERVICES

Karen Feinberg is a freelance writer/editor who works in her own home. She writes for businesses, organizations, and individuals who do not have the skill or the time to do their own writing. As an editor she corrects and makes sense of what others have written while getting paid well for doing it. Typical writing assignments include sales letters, handbills, ads, brochures, newsletters, catalogs, ghost-written articles, speeches, and how-to directions. Editing work includes correcting and re-writing articles, technical papers, and books. When starting out, you can't pick and choose. Specialization comes later.

Freelance writers often specialize in advertising copywriting, radio and television commercial scripts, and direct mail. Some write brochures, catalogs, and other sales literature.

Finding Assignments

Getting started can be tough. You have to sell yourself and constantly "ask for the order." That means writing letters, making appointments and cold calls. Logical persons to approach for writing assignments include: executives in charge of advertising, public relations, marketing, and sales; store owners and operators; editors of company and institutional publications; and anyone involved with communications.

Make yourself known and leave your card with anyone you think might need your writing help. Show examples of your work if you have them. Make up a portfolio or brochure describing your services which you can include with a letter and leave behind when you make a call. Writers like Feinberg have also discovered that much of their business comes by word of mouth.

Feinberg tried advertising in the business pages of the daily newspaper. The little one-inch-by-two-column ad brought her some attention, but not enough. That led her to try inexpensive ads in professional journals. Now Feinberg gets much of her work from professionals in the fields of criminal justice, health, and social services who want to publish articles about their work, but need someone to edit their material.

What to Charge

You will probably charge most of your work by the job, but you'll also need an hourly rate to base your charges on. To know in advance how long a job will take, make your best guess and then double it. Don't be afraid to ask other freelancers what they charge. Ask advertising agency people and publication editors what they pay for services such as yours. An excellent guide for pricing is published in *Writer's Market*, available in libraries and bookstores.

A variety of rates have been compiled which should only be used as a guideline. Rates will vary depending on the local economy, the reputation of the writer and competition:

Ads	$75-150
Sales letters	$125-200
Ghost-written articles	$75-100 per typed page
Speeches	$25 a minute
Brochures and catalogs	$50-75 per printed page
Newsletters	$75-100 per printed page
Editing	$10-25 an hour
Hourly creative rate	$25-45 an hour

Start-Up Costs

If you want to be a writer for hire, your initial investment can be as small as $500. Some of the basic equipment required includes: a typewriter, a telephone, a dictionary, basic office supplies, business cards, and a space to work in. After the money starts coming in you can invest in files, a desk, a word processor with a letter-quality printer and so forth. From the beginning you must keep books, carefully recording all your income and expenses including auto mileage. You'll be able to deduct office expenses from your income tax, but follow the IRS's rules.

Persistence Pays

When Feinberg started out, she had some small savings

to fall back on, but it still meant a period of belt-tightening for her and her husband. It is necessary to have resources to live on for several months when starting out because your first income may not come for three months or more. The standard advice to anyone with a steady job is keep it until you prove you can be successfully self-employed. Do your freelancing after regular work hours. Freelancers call it "moonlighting." No one should go into freelance writing expecting to make a fortune, but you can make a good living if you put time and effort into it.

Feinberg has been freelancing for five years and her business has grown to the point where she has had to turn down work. At any one time, Feinberg will have as many as twenty jobs in various stages of completion. In order to keep her clients happy, Feinberg maintains regular business hours and always sticks to her deadlines.

It won't be long before you as a freelance writer will come to a crossroads. A client will ask: "Can you illustrate this job? Get it in type? Get it printed? Can you write, produce and place an ad for me?" As soon as you say "yes" you are no longer exclusively a freelance writer, but a one-person creative studio or advertising agency. This is what many freelancers hope will happen. You are on your way to expanding your business if you decide to buy art, type, printing, and place advertising in addition to your writing. You are also in a situation that requires much more working capital and has greater risks.

Feinberg has been careful to keep services she buys to a minimum, preferring to devote her time to writing and editing. "I have more freedom this way," says Feinberg. "I do what I like, and I get paid for it."

Rules for Success

1. Do the best work you are capable of doing.
2. Be honest. If you can't deliver work when it is wanted, say so. Instead of losing the job, you'll probably get a longer deadline.
3. Explain in the beginning what the job will entail, including your fee.
4. Organize your time. Don't try to do too much.
5. Be firm. Don't let anyone intimidate you into lowering a fee, or doing what you don't want to do.
6. Never do work on speculation. The exception may be writing you do for publication under your own name.
7. Don't leave messages with children.
8. Beware of unbalanced and unreliable types; they are probably slow pay or no pay.
9. Find time to relax.
10. Don't give up.

Van Caldwell

WEDDING CONSULTANT

Every year the number of women in the work force increases. Many of these career women are brides and mothers of brides, the traditional wedding planners. Because the engaged couple and their families often don't have enough time to spend on making the wedding arrangements, wedding consultants are being hired to step-in.

Wedding consulting is a relatively new home business that already is meeting heavy demand. "We provide a service to the women who don't have the time to plan a wedding or just want a professional to do some of the harder planning," says Minna-Rea Friedman, a wedding consultant and owner of Weddings and Parties Unlimited.

"Planning a wedding need not be limited to finding a location for the reception," explains Mary Gerace, owner of Weddings to Remember, another wedding consulting firm. "Wedding planners can aid in everything from the engagement announcement to finding the newlyweds the ideal honeymoon retreat."

How to Start, What to Offer

Before you start your business, you should set goals and limits. The limits refer to the type of service that will be offered. Gerace contends that it is preferable to tell a bride that you cannot provide a certain service, than to attempt something you are not prepared to work on. "Offer the bride alternatives that you can provide or other outlets that can deliver exactly what the bride wants," Gerace says.

Contact banquet halls and caterers in the area, view the facilities, sample food, and observe a wedding in progress, taking note of service, staff, seating, and other details. Narrow down the list of facilities you may choose to recommend and work with than to offer alternatives you are unsure of.

Among the criteria used to evaluate halls should be:

- Location—easy access to expressways and airports.

- Price and value—caterers of different price ranges should be represented to give the couple some options.

- Cleanliness and atmosphere—a facility that is not clean or appealing to the eye will not sell a bride.

- Food quality—cheap is not necessarily best.

- Staffing—employees should be courteous, friendly, and plentiful.

Although the caterers and banquet halls you select will form the core of your recommendation list, a bride will often already have an idea of what she would like. Gerace explained that she has often worked with a bride to find a new location that fits the bride's specifications, and then adds that location to the recommendation list.

"Flower shops and bridal gown shops are another area that the consultant should thoroughly research. Shops with large selections and reputations for reliability should be considered first. This does not mean that small shops should be ignored," Gerace explains. "Often a small shop will be more receptive to working with a consultant, and will provide quality and personal attention that may be lacking in a large or chain store." Friedman has also made contacts with tuxedo rental stores and livery rentals so her service can assist the groom-to-be as well.

Using Referrals

"Many times a referral type of service is set up. Each time an outlet sends a bride to your consulting firm a referral fee can be paid. Fees vary based on the size of the job received or the number of clients referred in a given time period," says Gerace. Shops will often offer discounts to the consultant, or the consultant may be able to negotiate a lower price than the bride, because the shop would like repeat business from the consultant. "Wedding consultants not only save the future bride a lot of headaches and time, but the price for the wedding will probably be lower," says Friedman.

Secondary outlets that the consulting firm should seek out include bands and DJs, bakeries, printers, photographers, bridal accessory suppliers, and jewelers. Because the quality of these services is often a matter of individual taste—one band will not satisfy everyone's need for music, nor will one bakery please everyone's palate—the best method for handling these areas is to begin a file of stores and suppliers, complete with services offered and price ranges.

Target Your Market

Gerace says that wedding consultants can target a particular market or group. Perhaps you will choose to specialize in limited-budget weddings, or work with theme weddings in offbeat locations. Once you find your niche in the market, you can always expand and include more options in your services.

Because this type of business is relatively new, many people will not know about the availability of your service. The solution is to market yourself and your service. The easiest and cheapest form of advertising, according to both Gerace and Friedman, is your professional contacts: the bridal shops, florists, caterers, and banquet halls. Remind your contacts that referrals work both ways, and the more business you have, the more business they will have. Most wedding consultants list their business in the telephone directory under weddings or party planners. However, some are also affiliated with a dress shop or florist for added exposure.

Bridal magazines are another outlet for advertising. While this form of advertising may be more costly than newspapers, the magazines are read exclusively by women preparing weddings. Your target market is being reached and none of your advertising dollar is being wasted on unconcerned readers.

Bridal shows also attract a large audience and are well worth the costs involved. Typically these shows combine advertising booths with a bridal fashion show, raffles for trips or shopping sprees, and other information for the bride-to-be. At these shows, ad books are provided which are often kept as references by the bride. Shows of this sort are typically held four times a year and are sponsored by a department store, hotel, or shopping mall.

Working With the Bride

Once a bride comes to your firm, it is important to pinpoint her needs and wants, her tastes, and available budget, Gerace advises. If you are the first stop on the bride's planning route, it will be necessary to work with the bride to set up a wish list.

The easiest and most effective way to start working with a bride-to-be is through a well-worded questionnaire. Bridal party size, type of reception, and size of guest list should all be summarized on one sheet along with ceremony, special details, color schemes, preferred locations, and other information. Once you and the bride have discussed ideas and budget, you can go to work coordinating the plans.

The most important thing to remember, Friedman points out, is that each bride is special and has her own ideas and dreams. Your function is to help all those dreams materialize, not to create a standard wedding to sell to every bride. The wedding consulting business takes a lot of hard work, a great deal of creativity, and patience.

While the possibilities and opportunities for this business are endless, the consultant should still set a plan for growth and development. "The best part of being a wedding consultant is helping to make one of the happiest days in a couple's life even happier," Gerace concludes.

Wendy Hopps and William Ball

Part Six:

8 REPAIR & MAINTENANCE BUSINESSES

BICYCLE REPAIR

Combining high-tech with personalized service has built a successful business and satisfying lifestyle for Jim Kozel, a thirty-eight-year-old "bicycle doctor who makes house calls." Kozel's place of business is a van equipped with a cellular phone and more tools and spare parts than can be found in most bicycle shops. He uses a computer to target his customers and to provide them with a high degree of personal service often lost in the pressure of today's business.

Focusing on high-profit areas, Kozel repairs bicycles at his customers' homes where they can look over his shoulder and pick up maintenance tips. Families are the bread and butter of his business, while about 8 percent of his customers are serious riders who require custom work.

Pulling up in a customer's driveway, Kozel jumps out of his van and pulls up the rear door to reveal a three-foot-deep workshop containing a parts washer, two mechanics' tool chests, and a removable stand on which to mount the ailing bike. Working directly behind the van, he is within easy reach of his tools. Between this work area and the front seat of the car, there is storage space for tires, tubes, spokes, handlebars, saddles, and wheels.

Besides saving his clients the hassle of transporting their crippled bicycles to a shop, Kozel develops a personal relationship with them, often listening to their problems as he works. He explains what he's doing, tells them how they can take better care of their bikes, and watches them ride after he's finished the job. He cured one man's leg cramps by noting that he curled his toes as he pedaled.

An avid bicycle rider himself, Kozel left his "golden handcuff" salary as an account executive and moved to Colorado where he could ride in the Rocky Mountains. "I thought about what I was good at that would make money," he recalls. "Ever since my dad let me work in his shop as a kid, I've liked to build things. I love bicycling, and I've built and rebuilt my bikes. And I really like people. This kind of analysis led to something I trust: a BFO— Blinding Flash of the Obvious."

Not one to be dazzled by high-gross profit figures, which are often dissipated in overhead costs, he has always had a net. In an average year he earns $26,000 on a gross of $40,000. Instead of saddling himself with rental space and utility costs when he began operations in 1986, he made a down payment of $1,600 on a $10,000 van. He invested $6,000 in tools and spare parts, and took out a one-sixth-page advertisement in the *Yellow Pages* for $240 a month.

Since then, he has cut back on the ad, which as a repair business was listed after dealers who also make repairs. Finger-walkers usually stopped at the D's before they came to his ad, and he barely broke even on costs. He now has a half-inch ad in the metropolitan Denver directory and a two-inch column in each of the area books where he operates, at a cost of $150 a month.

His first summer, he also ran a weekly $200 quarter-page ad in a giveaway newspaper widely read as an entertainment guide. It paid off handsomely by attracting the attention of a *Denver Post* reporter, largely because of the logo, which Kozel designed himself. Instead of the conventional bicycle, it's a physician's head wearing a mirror shaped like a bicycle wheel.

Kozel's knack for public relations has resulted in a total of five display stories in both major Denver newspapers, and two features on a local radio station. While he has never sent out a press release or phoned a reporter, he is always aware of publicity, and the nature of his business attracts it.

"My customers know a lot of people, and they tell their friends about the great time they had drinking coffee with the bicycle doctor while he fixed their bike. The word gets around, and pretty soon someone from the media is calling me," he explains. His van also affords good picture possibilities, since it can show him doing things in an interesting setting. As his business grew, his reputation spread by word of mouth, and the return on his newspaper ad decreased. He has since been able to drive his costs down further by discontinuing it.

Other expenses include gas, which runs under $100 a month, and van repairs, which are less than $400 a year including oil and snow tires. His cellular phone bill varies from under $100 in the winter off-season to $300 during busy months. He spends about $8,000 a year on parts. With these costs, he is able to stay competitive with the better bike shops, charging, for example, $39 for a tune-up. Friendly relations with local dealers result in mutual referrals.

Two capital expenses were clearly justified: his computer and his cellular telephone. Before buying the phone, he and his wife were spending two hours every night returning calls that had accumulated on their home answering machine. The phone, which cost $800 with an extra battery (plus charges of 35¢ a minute for both incoming and outgoing calls), allows Kozel to make and receive calls anywhere he goes.

Kozel has 1,400 clients in his computer database, most

of them repeats. He can call up their record in an instant and know their bike history when he talks to them. It has also helped him narrow his territory to areas in which he has higher average sales. When he started out, he sometimes drove as much as forty miles to service one bike. Now he can concentrate on higher profit custom work or families with several bikes that may need work at one time.

With his computer, he also puts out a newsletter twice a year that goes to the homes of 4,000 known bicycle riders. It offers tips on bicycle maintenance, how to get in shape for spring riding, and other information that keeps readers involved in the sport and makes it more enjoyable. It also advertises his own day-long Saturday seminars (breakfast and lunch included) on bicycle repairs and maintenance. The response in new business is better than 10 percent.

Adeline McConnell

CARPET REPAIR

If you are looking for a new career opportunity, a small Oregon company called Tronco, Inc., offers you a profitable career as a carpet repair technician. You can earn money and save money for homeowners, renters, and commercial facilities managers. No matter how stained or ripped the carpet might be, Tronco will teach you an easy, step-by-step method for carpet repair.

Carpeting is warm and beautiful, but it's an expensive investment. Smart people want to protect their investments. Tronco can show you how to save carpet replacement dollars, and how to protect your customer's investment.

"I started small," says Helen Tronrud, president of Tronco, Inc. "Thirty-nine years ago I began by reweaving fabric in Eau Claire, Wisconsin. My business has continued successfully, even though I have since moved to Oregon, and am now retufting carpets almost exclusively. It's easier than reweaving carpet. I've saved owners lots of money over the years. Now I'm showing others how to do it."

Helen has developed a kit that includes special equipment used to mend carpets. She claims that with the proper tools, anyone can be an expert. She teaches a special, step-by-step method of carpet repair. Damaged spots, such as burns from fireplace embers or cigarettes, and stains or chemical spills are no problem for her students to repair.

Carpets may have a replacement value of $500 to $2,500 or more. Tronco's complete kit of tools, and a comprehensive set of instructions allows the carpet to be repaired at a fraction of the cost. With some practice, you should be able to do a $100 repair job in less than one hour. If you need personal assistance, Helen can be reached by telephone.

The Repair Method

Helen has a foolproof method of burling and tufting carpeting. Little tufts of carpet are used from existing materials or remnants. Placing the tufts all around, she backs, plants, fastens, and tacks them with a special latex. Using a special retufter tool, she makes the perfect invisible Tronco repair. She does not use an iron, and no glue strips are involved. Color matching is no problem, as tufts come from the carpet being repaired.

"To make this invisible repair, you must have a precise set of tools," she says. "The carpet company craftsman will often cut out a square piece of carpet and patch it in with glue, making it an obvious and visible repair. Sometimes they won't repair the carpet at all. An invisible Tronco repair can be performed quickly and effortlessly," says Helen.

There is a big demand for people in this field. The industry has outgrown the number of existing repair technicians, according to the experts at Tronco. The job pays a minimum of twenty dollars an hour plus travel and expenses. Another selling point is that it's clean work, and you are liable to be busy all the time. "The kit I have prepared is complete, and anyone can learn this lifetime career," Helen points out.

The one special tool, the retufter, is manufactured and imported from Europe. It's not available in department or chain stores. The tools never need replacing, and no previous experience is necessary to learn how to use the tools. Additional supplies cost little. Although it's hard to believe, you won't find information about carpet repair in carpet stores. These drawbacks to the average consumer make this field even more lucrative for anyone wanting to be a carpet repairperson.

If you are interested in making your own hours, and securing your financial future, think about working for Tronco. If you work well with tools, and enjoy people, you'll be guaranteed success in your own carpet repair business. The cost of the kit is $89.95.

For free information, write: Tronco, 861 Arcadia Drive, Eugene, OR 97401.

Art Lamons

GLASS INSTALLATION

In the glass trade you never run out of work. As long as people live in houses and drive cars there will always be glass to be installed. "It's a pretty secure trade," says Alan Heaberlin, glass installer. If you are going to take the plunge and start your own business, isn't that what you really want—security? Heaberlin is the owner of Southwest Glass Service. He first started in the glass business as a "fill-in" when he owned his own picture framing service. When the framing business was slow he'd help out with glass work.

Learning the Basics

After about a year of working in glass installation part-time, Heaberlin realized that it would make more sense to work at it full-time. He hired someone to run the picture frame shop, went into the glass business, and eventually sold the frame shop.

"There's a lot of things involved in the glass business, and there are still some things I learn now," says Heaberlin. One of the ways he learned more about his trade was by working by contract for different shops. For instance, some shops would send him to Los Angeles for storefront work, something they didn't have in the smaller city he lived in. He also worked for a shop that did nothing but custom mirror work. He learned to do repairs on stained glass, too. When he was learning his craft, Heaberlin didn't limit himself. He learned as much as he could, followed his interests, and gained valuable experience.

Now, as an experienced glazier of sixteen years, he does a variety of work. He does window repairs for ordinary windows, rescreening, shower doors, mirrored wardrobe doors, dual-pane windows, storm windows, and auto glass. More and more people are conscientious about energy conservation, which means they want to replace their windows with dual-pane windows and storm windows. Repairing a dual-pane window is no easy trick. "It's not like an ordinary hack-out (fixing a broken window)," explains Heaberlin. "The units have to be manufactured." In dual-pane windows the space between the two pieces of glass is filled with a desiccate, or drying agent that keeps steam from appearing. So the process of making them is more involved—and higher priced.

When Heaberlin is called out to fix a broken window, the first thing he does is identify the type of material he is replacing, then he cleans up the mess. For protection he uses sturdy rubber gloves. They allow a better grip and protection from cuts. "Your best safety device is common sense," he advises. You never want to get underneath a broken piece of glass that is hanging.

Starting Costs

Starting costs vary. All of your basic tools, basic parts, and a month's supply of stock can run about $5,000 to $10,000. But it might not even cost that much. When Heaberlin was working with the other glass business he managed to buy many of the tools he would be needing. He had a homemade rack on the back of a pickup truck and worked out of his garage at home. He also says that many suppliers will not sell their product to you unless you have a full-time retail operation. This is in order to keep the fly-by-nighters out. If a bad job is done with the product, it can make a bad reputation for that supplier and everyone else who sells that product.

Advertising

Heaberlin advertises by newspaper, but says it is hard to tell if he gets a lot of business that way. He does feel it is good exposure to have his business name seen in the paper. The phone book is his best source of customers, and also word of mouth, and repeat business. It is a good idea to become known by the rest of the business community. A lot of your business will come from other business people. Heaberlin is a member of the board of directors of his local chamber of commerce. In this way he keeps in close contact with the other members of the business community and it pays off.

Installation Creativity

There are fifty different types of windows and they all have different requirements and specifications. "In the community that we live in, most of the windows are in aluminum sliding frames with a rubber spline," Heaberlin says. This is where creativity comes in. Many of the older windows are obsolete so the glazier may have to fabricate something to make it work. If it can't be done, an entirely new window must be installed. Sometimes that entails removing the stucco and painting it. In the long run the glazier may wind up doing carpentry and electrical work.

There can be a lot of other trades involved when working with glass.

Heaberlin makes his own screen doors by buying all of the raw materials and putting them together right in his shop. When it comes to repairing screen doors, he straightens the frame when possible and replaces the screen. At certain times of the year the glazier can go to property managers and real estate agents to get a contract for all of their screening.

Another thing that Heaberlin has been successful with is the repair and replacing of shower doors. In years past, obscure wire glass was used in doors, but this type of glass is not legal anymore so it must be replaced with tempered safety glass or a whole new unit must be installed. Because of the build-up of alkali and the decomposition of the frame, it may not be worth replacing the glass. Many times the opportunity for the sale of a new unit is there.

Auto Glass Business

"Auto glass is almost a whole business in itself," Heaberlin says. In the windy deserts of California, motorists find it necessary to replace their windshield on an average of once every other year. It is profitable to go to the various insurance agents in the community and let them know you are working on auto glass, since replacements are usually done through the insurance companies. He also restores antique car glass. Before 1948, automobiles weren't required to have safety glass, so many antique car owners have the windows replaced. Each time he replaces windows in an antique car, he makes a pattern of the window to save for future use.

Heaberlin makes a good profit with his business. As with any business, the longer you are established the more successful you will be and better able to get through the hard times. Expanding his business to include the building of dual-pane windows for sale to other glass shops is a move that he feels will be a profitable one.

Jo Ann M. Unger

HOME REPAIR

With all the uncertainty in the investment markets these days, it's difficult to know just where you should be putting your extra money. During this period of dubiety there is only one answer: invest in used and bruised houses. That's right, in structurally sound, but worn and dirty single-family homes.

There are two reasons for investing in these eyesores:

- They can be acquired below prevailing real estate prices.
- Once given the mandatory industrial strength clean-up, they can be sold at a handsome profit.

Why Invest Now?

There are three main reasons:

1. You can easily sell what you buy. To begin with, the cost of housing is constantly rising above the inflation rate. Individual wages are not. This continually lowers the Affordability Index, the

term bankers use to determine the percentage of home buyers who meet mortgage loan lending requirements in order to qualify for that loan. Today, only about 60 percent of the people who apply for loans qualify. This means that four out of ten people don't. These people—and there are millions of them—need clean, affordable property. You can provide it for them once you've cleaned up and fixed your used and bruised house.

2. It's easy to find them. You can find used and bruised houses everywhere and you won't face tremendous competition for them. That's because most people don't want to buy a less-than-new-anything—certainly not a dirty, used and bruised house, even if it only requires minor repairs and a good cleaning. You can therefore buy what other people don't want. That, of course, is very good for you.

3. You make money. Because used and bruised houses can be bought at least 25 percent below fair market value and, once touched up, they can bring prices above that value. It's hard not to earn a substantial profit.

Don't Throw Away the Classifieds

So what do you have to do to get in on this affordable investment alternative? Start with your local newspaper. The classified section is probably the fastest, least expensive, and usually the best source of information for house bargains. Start with the "For Sale By Owner" section. Buy only from desperate, motivated sellers. Like it or not, another person's problem is your opportunity. The key to this investment is acquiring houses from people who want to sell more desperately than you want to buy. These people usually are selling because of divorce, job transfer, a move, financial difficulties, bad health, or job loss.

How do you discover them? They're waving a flag. Check out these classified headlines: "Divorce Sale," "Leaving Town," "Job Transfer." These people are looking for you! Avoid "handyman" or "fixer" specials. Newcomers to this business often make a crucial mistake, misconstruing a "used and bruised" house with a "handyman" or "fixer" special. A "handyman's special" or "fixer" is often a nightmare. What looks to be a bargain when you see it in the paper is usually overpriced because it needs costly and time-consuming repairs to bring it up to its potential value.

Remember, "used and bruised" means just that. This house is dirty. Its floor coverings are worn. Windows may be broken. What it needs is a serious cleaning, followed by a cosmetic face-lift of fresh paint, new floor coverings, and other minor repairs. Nothing more.

How Much Should You Pay?

There are three methods of determining the true retail value of any house:

1. Investigate twenty-five to fifty houses which are for sale in your target area(s). You've got to know what property in the area sells for.

2. Visit your county courthouse to determine the

actual sales prices of recently sold houses in your area.

3. Compare your market research with the construction replacement cost used by insurance companies in your area. Ask your insurance agent or any local insurance company for this information. They use it on a daily basis to compute homeowner's coverage.

Now you've got a sense of what you should be paying in order to make a profit. It's just as important to know when to walk away from a house that looks good on the outside. What you must avoid is a house with major structural problems. They are the basis for real nightmares. Never assume a house is structurally sound regardless of how it looks, either inside or out. In addition, make sure your purchase contract always stipulates that the sale of the house is contingent on its passing a thorough inspection within seventy-two hours of the offer being signed.

Who should do the inspection? Try using retired tradespeople, unless you're a jack-of-all trades yourself. Why retired? Because they're not trying to sell you something you don't need. They need to check for problems in four general areas: structural, electrical, the plumbing system, and the heating and cooling system.

Negotiating to Sell When You Buy

Don't forget, you're not buying this house to live in. You're buying it to sell and make money. Negotiate to buy as if you were negotiating to sell today. Don't agree to any conditions that preclude your ability to sell the house right away.

Eliminate banks from every house you buy. Get the mortgage money anywhere but from standard banking institutions. You always want to avoid the mortgage loan disqualification process for two reasons: it takes too long and it's too expensive. Paying points alone can add thousands of dollars to your costs.

To achieve this objective, your used and bruised house should have one of these four types of nonqualifying assumable mortgages:

- Nonqualifying assumable Veterans Administration (VA) mortgage.

- Nonqualifying assumable Federal Housing Administration (FHA) mortgage.

- Nonqualifying assumable privately held mortgage.

- Owner (seller) financed mortgages for houses which are owned free and clear and have no mortgage.

Selling Your House in Thirty to Forty Days

Once you've got your house, start marketing it for an immediate profit. Here's what you should do:

1. Sell the house yourself. Place a professional looking "FOR SALE" sign on the property. Advertise your house for sale in your local newspapers.

2. Pay a fixed, flat fee. Use a flat-fee real estate company to help you sell your house. They only get paid a flat fee (about 25 percent of what conventional real estate agents charge) if and when they provide a buyer for the house.

3. Use a broker. Use real estate brokers to sell your house. Pay this broker a 3 percent sales commission, but only when the broker's prospect actually buys the property. Don't sign a listing agreement with any brokers.

Is This the Right Business for You?

You should consider this investment alternative only if you meet several important conditions:

- You've got to be good at negotiating.
- Good at finding the workers you'll need (unless you plan to do all the work yourself—a very heavy responsibility).
- Good at organization.

If you can do all this, investing in used and bruised houses is a very good way to make money, even if you have only a moderate amount to invest.

For More Information

How to Buy Used and Bruised Houses for Fast Profits by Thomas J. Lucier. Real Estate Publications, Inc., P.O. Box 20027, Tampa, FL 33622-0027. A step-by-step guide to what it takes to make money in affordable real estate; $19.95 postpaid.

Finding and Fixing Old Houses. E.A. Morgan Publishing Co., P.O. Box 1375, Huntington, NY 11743; $10.95

Thomas J. Lucier

LANDSCAPE MAINTENANCE

Gail Borling always finds the greenest grass on her side of the fence. Borling, owner of Gail's Gardening of Gig Harbor, Washington, maintains the grounds of four major condominium complexes in addition to wielding her green thumb for some fifty to sixty residential customers on a weekly or otherwise regular basis.

What began for Borling as a love for the outdoors and a desire to be in business for herself, has grown into an $80,000-plus yearly business. Others with similar aptitudes in horticulture and business management may find the economic climate equally promising for starting a landscape maintenance business of their own. Nationally, consumers are spending more each year on services, and the yard is one of the places where that money is going. But before you run out and buy a lawn mower and a pickup truck, consider some of the elements that led to Borling's success.

Learn Now, Earn Later

Borling discovered gardening back in her college days, when she took a job tending lawns at a local golf course. She enjoyed the work, and began then and there to take steps to eventually go into a lawn care business for herself; she changed her major to turf management and took a minor in business. Even if you cannot pursue a college degree, you can gain valuable knowledge and experience by taking classes in horticulture at a local vocational school or community college. Your county extension services may offer training as a master gardener in return for a certain number of hours in community service acting as a resource person to the public. Above all, experience in the field through work at a garden center, golf course, or for another gardener is the best training available to the potential entrepreneur.

Borling's preparation continued after college when she began working at a garden center in the Midwest. She gained invaluable experience working with the public, which she builds upon every day now in her business. It was at the garden center where Borling met her husband, Bob Rowan. Soon after they were married, the couple moved across country and settled in Gig Harbor where they found easy access to the outdoor recreation they enjoyed, as well as a level of affluence conducive to starting a service business.

Borling worked for another year at a nearby golf course, gaining knowledge of local gardening needs before launching into her own business. She began conservatively by purchasing two inexpensive homeowner-type lawn mowers, buying a used string trimmer, and commandeering the small pickup truck she had been using in her commutes to the golf course.

She advertised in the local paper, emphasizing her horticultural background, and promoted her business through the local garden center where her husband had found employment. Work began to come in and Borling was at last managing her own full-time lawn care business.

Build a Strong Customer Base

The first off-season was difficult, but Borling quickly built up a broad customer base to carry the business through the winter months. She has evened out her income through a pro-rated, year-round billing system for some of her customers. She also can now schedule many landscape projects for the winter and fall. Borling continually stresses the importance of remaining flexible to her customers' needs. By maintaining a close relationship with her clients, Borling has created a steady customer base from which she derives most of her income. She asks her customers what they prefer, and then seeks to provide it. "I've been able to keep the majority of my clients from the beginning," says Borling. "I think it's how you deal with the customer. Working flexibility into the program is essential for keeping long-term relationships with your clients—as long as they are willing to pay for it, and as long as it's something that I'm good at."

Keeping the business end of what she does thriving requires much the same care as the yards and landscapes she tends. Her formula for continued success involves flexibility with her customers, and a constant eye for efficiency, especially in the management of her work force.

By experimenting with different configurations of work crews, Borling discovered that her direct involvement with the crews improved her profitability. "I get out and work on the job at least half a day, every day," says Borling. "When I had seven employees, I spent the whole day being manager, and I would have to depend on someone else to run the crew. Now I depend more on each of the guys on the crew instead of someone who's overseeing them." Last year, Borling was able to maintain the same annual income that she had for the past few years, but she reduced the amount of employees from seven down to four.

Paring down the work force improved Borling's profits. Offering services that conform to what customers need has also contributed to her success. Though she stresses the importance of flexibility with her customers, Borling has purposely limited the kinds of jobs she will do. "I found that we started to make money when we took jobs that we were good at," says Borling. "There was a point at the beginning of the business where we had to take any and all work that came our way just to pay the bills. But now we've developed somewhat of a reputation for doing certain things, and we try to stick to that."

Range of Services

The demand for landscaping services can range anywhere from the design and construction of a landscape to watering the flowers for a client on vacation. Not all tasks provide a good return for your time, and some things may be beyond your expertise. Landscape construction, for instance, requires a contractor's license and special bonding; it should not be attempted by a beginner. Borling has built her business predominately on maintenance of existing landscapes. It is important to determine the parameters of the service you will provide in order to avoid getting sidetracked by the demand into less-than-productive areas.

One of the most profitable services is lawn mowing, according to Borling. "You can make pretty good money mowing lawns if you do certain things such as keeping your accounts close together, and also cutting lawns that are easy and quick to do," says Borling.

A lawn business can be easily started on a part-time basis with just a few customers. Start-up costs are low, especially if you own a pickup truck already. In the beginning, an inexpensive homeowner's lawn mower and a gas-powered string trimmer will get you started for less than $400. Later you will want to upgrade to a commercial lawn mower because of its power in wet grass, but at first the inexpensive machine will start earning you some part-time income.

Lush lawns and trim landscapes mean a year-round income for Borling, despite the somewhat seasonal nature of her business. Her edge in the business is a steady customer base, nurtured through reliable service, from which she derives most of her income. But steady work is not the only advantage she enjoys from providing a respected, in-demand service.

David Boyd

MOBILE SHARPENING SERVICE

You may have seen ads in magazines for machines that can sharpen saw blades, knives, and scissors. With these machines, they say, you can open a sharpening service in your neighborhood. There are many such shops around the country, and most of them do quite well, making a modest full-time income or a good part-time income. One way to optimize revenue from such a business is to bring the service to the customer, using a van or motorhome—a *mobile* sharpening service.

The reason many shop-based businesses only make a modest full-time income is that they limit themselves to just saw blades and lawn mower blades. Yet the percentage of population that owns saws is quite small; replacement blades are relatively cheap. Lawn mowers are too big and awkward for anyone to bring into the shop; most people would not attempt to remove a blade.

Although these blades can easily be accommodated by a mobile sharpening service, the items most in need of service are the common bread knife, carving knife, and other kitchen utensils. In a mini-survey, conducted by the author, out of 100 houses called, 82 wanted their knives sharpened. Next were scissors, then lawn mower blades, and last of all were saws and workshop items. This clearly shows what is needed—and always the formula for success is to find a need and fill it.

Now that you know the facts and reason to start a profitable mobile sharpening business, here's how to begin.

Tools and Machinery

There are several good machines on the market that use emeries and whetstones, priced at around $100, and they give excellent results. Most use 100-horsepower motors and 110 volts. A flat-faced sanding disk six inches in diameter using fine-grade garnet paper will sharpen knives and scissors.

You will probably need a generator, producing 1,000 watts, for your van or motorhome. Build a small, sturdy table and mount your tools where they can be ready to use. Also, have a metal container for water, as you must not let the knives and other utensils become overheated, dulling the edge. Any handyman can rig this up for not more than $200. Other miscellaneous items you'll need to start are

1,000 heavy envelope-type bags measuring about 6" x 11"; if you can afford it, have them printed with the name of your firm and its home address and phone number. There should also be space on the back or a separate tag for the purpose, on which to write your customer's name, address, phone number, type of items, charge per item, and total charge. Have a price chart written up that lists the charges for the sharpening of each item: knives, 50¢; scissors, $1; etc.

Pick out a good residential neighborhood and perhaps hire two young people. Have them go to each house, introduce themselves, and ask if they can leave a bag, and collect it back in about half an hour. You will find that up to 80 percent of those called on will be happy to return the bag filled with items to be sharpened. Have them fill out their name and address on the bag, and you have a complete record that will avert any mixups.

If the customer requests lawn mower-blade sharpening, offer to remove the blade from his lawnmower, sharpen it, and replace the blade all for a modest fee.

Park your motor home or van in a central location and you will have your two agents bringing you bags of items as fast as you can handle them. This is slow work: that is, it takes a long time to cover a city or even a good-sized town, so about twice a year is as often as your rig will be in a particular neighborhood. Once you have been working this method for some time, you will find more and more people requesting service between calls. It now makes sense to set up a sharpening shop. Every day your rig is working a neighborhood, you are doing two things: first, you are making a good income, and second, you are leaving a valuable advertisement each time you return a bag of sharpened items. This will bring your shop a steady stream of customers.

In apartment buildings, call on the superintendent or landlord first, and get his or her permission to call on the apartment tenants (a few bucks sometimes helps). He will usually let you park in the apartment parking lot. Set up and operate every day. You won't be sitting and waiting for customers, and you will show a solid profit each and every day.

Sharpening Equipment

Foley-Belsaw Co., 6301 Equitable Rd., Kansas City, MO 64120. Offers a free Fact Kit explaining how to start your own business.

H. K. King

PHONE INSTALLATION

Bob Jones needed a telephone extension put in his home, but when he called the phone company he was told that he'd have to wait about thirty days to be serviced. Jones did not want to wait a month just to get an extension, so he decided that he would do the job himself. It sounds too simple to be true, but this is what motivated Jones to start his own telephone extension business. Today, he is enjoying his business and the profits it reaps. Jones began with barely any knowledge about how telephones work; he had only a genuine interest in electronics. He learned his business from scratch—and so can you.

Jones began his research by gathering information on how to start a business by talking to people with experience. Then he investigated the field of telephone installation by reading articles on the topic in "handyman"-type magazines. By doing all of this preliminary work, Jones was in a better position to decide whether or not this was the right business for him.

After committing himself to the venture, Jones visited a local electronics store that carried a book which contained information he would need, such as step-by-step instructions, helpful hints, short cuts for running a line through walls, installing wiring, and running multiple lines. Not only did Jones have to learn his trade, but he also needed to learn the legalities of operating this type of business. After purchasing his business license he contacted the State Board of Licenses to find out what services he was and wasn't allowed to perform. "They said I could do any job up to $199. After that I'd have to get a low-voltage electrician's license," says Jones. Since Jones has never done a job over $199, he decided not to get an electrician's license.

Profits and Expenses

Jones charges one low price for installation, parts, and labor. For each extension he charges $19.95, while Contel of California—the area's phone utility—charges $49.50. "I can usually install a phone for one-third to one-fourth less than the phone company does it, and I'll come out the same day or the next day after you call," says Jones.

As for expenses, Jones was fortunate in that he already owned many of the needed tools, but there were some pieces of equipment he had to purchase especially for his phone business: a regular telephone with alligator clips on the end, and an in-line telephone meter. The telephone with alligator clips is used outside the home to check the ring; an in-line telephone meter is used to check the polarity and the ring-through on the line.

Jones discovered that three different sizes of ladders are needed: an extension ladder, a six-foot ladder, and a step ladder. The six-foot ladder is used for running wire under doorways inside the house and under eaves outside the house. The extension is used for double-story dwellings or apartments. Some of the other necessary tools include a battery-operated portable drill and a special staple gun. A battery-operated drill makes it easy to drill holes in any location, inside or out, without having to find an AC power source. The staple gun, Arrow model T-28, uses round staples of two different colors—beige and uncolored—to fasten phone wire to room baseboard and molding. Other miscellaneous tools are wire cutters, strippers, and screwdrivers. "When all the initial equipment was bought, it totalled around $150 to $200," says Jones.

In order to cut down on the cost of supplies, Jones wrote to an electronics company. He was sent their catalog and was able to order his supplies for 50 percent less than he would have paid in a retail store in his area. Jones also finds it economical to buy parts on sale and stock up. Then he doesn't have to worry about not having the parts when he needs them.

Safety

It is not a risky job as far as safety goes, but Jones advises that you keep in mind the following safety tips when on a job:

- If you are running wire through the attic be careful not to step through the ceiling.

- If you are drilling through a wall, be certain you are not drilling through a natural gas pipe or electrical wires.

- Double-check to see if there are any plug-ins under the beam you are drilling into by going outside and looking in.

Advertising

Jones says the best way to get started in the business is to do jobs for friends and relatives for the initial experience and exposure. Many of his friends were satisfied with their extension and told other friends about the business. They were pleased with the quality of the workmanship, the speed with which they were able to get their new phone working, and the price in view of what the phone company was charging. As a result, Jones used hardly any advertising to get his business off the ground. "Most of my business comes from word of mouth and business cards that I hand out," says Jones.

Jones has had few complaint callbacks on the jobs he has done. When he does get a call for repair work, it is usually to replace lines that have been accidentally pulled from the wall or to replace cords that have been pulled on or kinked too much and must be replaced.

Jones is quite content with this business he has started and he makes the extra income he needs. By following Jones' example, perhaps phone installation could also be your line.

Jo Ann M. Unger

SMALL ENGINE REPAIR

"**K**eep believing that you can get better and there are ways to improve what you're doing." For twelve years this has been the motto of Bob Shetler and John Magee, owners of Omega Maintenance. Just a short distance from downtown Los Angeles, this thriving business has been grossing $150,000 a year. It wasn't always that way, however. Bob and John started their business from a home garage with only twenty-five customers.

"I really had no background at all in small engine repair," says John. "So it was quite an adjustment for me." Bob, on the other hand, had always tinkered with small engines, mini-bikes, and lawn mowers since he was a boy. In high school, he took a school/work training course in small engine repair and learned most of what he would use in his business.

John and Bob started their business with basic mechanics' tools: wrenches, sockets, screwdrivers, and valve kits. Soon after, they added sharpening equipment and a welder. Most of their equipment was purchased at reduced rates from businesses that were disbanding. John estimates that anyone interested in going into this business needs about $1,000 for tools.

Today, John and Bob repair lawn mowers, chain saws, weed eaters, rototillers, edgers, and gasoline-powered engines. They currently employ one other full-time person. John does the paperwork, orders parts, does mechanical work, and takes care of daily business-related matters.

Safety is paramount when working with small engines. Many of the distributors offer classes to help repairmen learn how to use their equipment. Some of these companies also provide video tapes that can be viewed and referred to when problems arise in repairing equipment.

"Safety classes are a must," says John. "They are very helpful in aiding you with the basics, and in showing you what to look for when you are doing repairs." John suggests that you purchase the following items to guarantee your safety around the shop: long pants, steel-toed boots, and goggles.

John and Bob spend $500 to $800 a year on advertising. They use the *Yellow Pages*, and have found that it draws a large percentage of their customers. They also run large ads in three different directories in their area. "There are several phone books that combine different cities in our area. This really works for us," John explains. "We don't advertise with the mailers or newspapers unless we are trying to highlight a sale item."

Sales comprise a large part of John and Bob's income. Besides offering small gas-powered engine equipment, they are dealers for several well-known companies. Many of their customers do a lot of their own repairs and come to the shop to buy the parts they need. "We deal with twenty different distributors," John says. "Some of them sell new units and parts and some only sell parts."

Monthly expenditures for parts varies from season to season. John and Bob spend a lot more for parts during the spring and summer months. In fact, the repair of lawn mowers outweighs all of their other repair jobs four to one. In the springtime they spend approximately $1,500 to $2,000 a month on parts.

Because Bob and John don't overlook the little details of their business they haven't had too many complaints.

"We ask our customers to tell us if they aren't happy with our work," John says. "We like the feedback, because we feel this helps us to improve." No doubt it is their attention to detail that has made Omega so successful. Many businesses tend to lose the personal touch when they become prosperous. Bob and John have been careful not to let that happen.

"You have to do more than just sell the customer a product. You have to show them that you value their business," says John. "It's very important that you don't lose that along the way."

Sources

If you are interested in where to find small engine parts distributors, contact the following:

Pacific West Stihl, Inc., 264 Winheld Circle, Corona, CA 91720; (714) 736-8855.

Bee Tee Equipment Sales, Inc., 21075 Alexander Ct., P.O. Box 3037, Hayward, CA 94540.

Rotary Corporation, 617 Terrace Way, P.O. Box 248, San Dimas, CA 91773.

Home Study

Foley-Belsaw Institute, 6301 Equitable Rd., Kansas City, MO 64120. Home study course includes manuals, tools, and 4 h.p. engine. Free details.

NRI Schools, McGraw-Hill Continuing Education Center, 4401 Connecticut Ave., Washington, D.C. 20008. Home study course on Small Engine Repair; free catalog.

Jo Ann M. Unger

INDEX